INSEARCH
ENGLISH

PREPARE FOR **IELTS**
SKILLS AND STRATEGIES

Book One
LISTENING AND SPEAKING

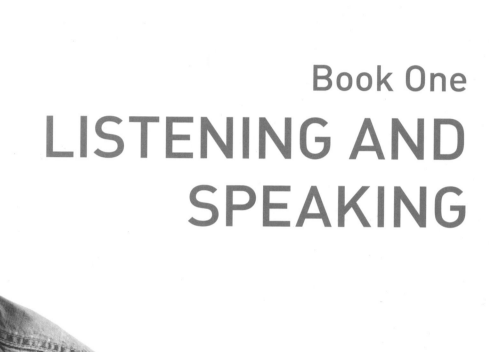

UNIVERSITY OF
TECHNOLOGY SYDNEY

INSEARCH UTS

Level 2, 187 Thomas Street

Sydney NSW 2000 Australia

www.insearch.edu.au

Copyright © 2007 INSEARCH UTS

Produced by the Publications Department of INSEARCH UTS

National Library of Australia
Cataloguing-in-Publication data

Prepare for IELTS: Skills and Strategies Book One: Listening and Speaking

ISBN 978-0-9085-3730-3

1.International English Language Testing System (IELTS)
2.English language—Examinations, questions, etc
3.English language—Textbooks for foreign speakers

I.   INSEARCH UTS
II. UTS International.
III. Title
IV. Title: Prepare for International English Language Testing System
V. Title: Prepare for IELTS

Edition Co-ordinator	Rae de Rooy
Consultants	David Larbalestier, Anna Shymkiw
Book Design	Stuart Gibson,
	Book Design Australia, www.bookdesign.com.au
Cover Design	EKH Branding House, www.ekhbranding.com.au
Layout	Norman Baptista, Natalie Wallis
Line Illustrations	Pam Horsnell
Diagrams	Stuart Gibson and Simon Leong
Photography	iStockPhoto
Print Production	Southwood Press, www.southwoodpress.com.au
Proofreaders	Tamara Pruze, Kristina Schulz, Brett Johnson,
	Kirill Shlenskiy, Matt Townsley

CONTENTS

NEW
UPDATED
FOR NEW
2006 WRITING
RUBRICS

WHY CHOOSE

→ Developed by **IELTS experts**

→ Covers all four parts of the IELTS test:
  LISTENING, READING, WRITING and **SPEAKING**

→ All tasks have been comprehensively
  tested in the classroom

→ Practical **hints** and **tips**

→ Logical layout with clear explanations

THIS SERIES?

→ Relevant information and tasks

→ Full **answer key** and **transcripts**

→ Sample writing answers

→ A comprehensive **variety** of
  question types

"As I knew that IELTS is a fairly difficult test,
I was a bit worried about the strategies I had
to know in order to be successful. Speaking
English is one thing, but the other is knowing
how to tackle the test itself."

FILIP ZAHRADNIK, SLOVAKIA

NEW:DIRECTION

Proudly published by

INSEARCH
ENGLISH

INSEARCH PROVIDES COURSES THAT LEAD TO UNIVERSITY DEGREES AND OTHER QUALIFICATIONS ACROSS A BROAD RANGE OF DISCIPLINES

→ As a provider of innovative language and academic pathways to university studies, INSEARCH is a leading institution of its type and teaching English is the cornerstone of its success. INSEARCH has a history of expertise in IELTS preparation, both within Australia and through its global network.

AUSTRALIA

→ Located in central Sydney, INSEARCH offers a wide range of IELTS preparation courses to suit different needs and is the provider of academic pathways to the University of Technology Sydney (UTS), one of the largest IELTS test centres in the world.

VIETNAM

→ INSEARCH operates the Australian Centre for Education and Training with joint venture partner, IDP Education Australia. A wide range of IELTS preparation courses, including customised corporate courses, are offered at both the Hanoi and Ho Chi Minh City locations. Both centres also offer pathway courses to IELTS. This option allows students not ready to sit the IELTS test to receive more preparatory tuition and optimise their preparation time.

→ IDP Education Australia is an approved IELTS test centre in both Hanoi and Ho Chi Minh City.

INDONESIA

→ The Australia Centre Medan is operated by INSEARCH. The centre offers a variety of English courses, including IELTS preparation, and is also an IELTS test centre.

THAILAND

→ INSEARCH operates the Australia Centre Chiang Mai where candidates may enrol in IELTS preparation courses and, as an approved IELTS test centre, may also register for and sit the IELTS test.

CHINA

→ INSEARCH also operates the Sydney Institute of Language and Commerce (SILC) in partnership with, and on the three campuses of, Shanghai University. SILC offers academic English preparation courses as well as diplomas in business and commerce, IT and communication.

UNITED KINGDOM

→ INSEARCH offers a range of English language courses and provides accredited academic pathway courses for entry into the second year of study (business and computer science) at the University of Essex.

courses@insearch.edu.au

www.insearch.edu.au

CRICOS provider code: 00859D

UTS:
SYDNEY'S
CITY UNIVERSITY

SYDNEY'S CITY
UNIVERSITY, THE
UNIVERSITY OF
TECHNOLOGY, SYDNEY
(UTS) REFLECTS THE
CITY AROUND IT:
MODERN, DIVERSE
AND PROGRESSIVE.

UNIVERSITY OF
TECHNOLOGY SYDNEY

→ BUSINESS
→ DESIGN, ARCHITECTURE AND BUILDING
→ EDUCATION
→ ENGINEERING
→ HUMANITIES AND SOCIAL SCIENCES
→ INFORMATION TECHNOLOGY
→ LAW
→ NURSING, MIDWIFERY AND HEALTH
→ SCIENCE
→ INTERNATIONAL STUDIES

→ Delivering professionally focused courses and topical research, UTS offers practical education with an international perspective. It is this unique combination of practicality, international awareness and city culture which distinguishes UTS from other universities. Offering more than 100 undergraduate and 200 postgraduate courses, UTS is much more than a technical university.

→ As one of Australia's largest and most respected universities, UTS attracts students from all over the world. The University encourages international interaction, fostering worldwide student exchanges and partnerships with over 110 universities in 24 countries. A multicultural mix of more than 30,000 students, including over 6,000 international students from 115 countries have chosen UTS because it offers:

→ CAREER-RELEVANT EDUCATION
→ TEACHING EXCELLENCE
→ A DIVERSE RANGE OF COURSES
→ EXCELLENT GRADUATE OUTCOMES
→ A MULTICULTURAL MIX OF STUDENTS
→ EXCELLENT FACILITIES AND STUDENT SERVICES
→ A UNIQUE EXPERIENCE OF AUSTRALIA

international@uts.edu.au
www.uts.edu.au/international/

CRICOS provider code: 00099F

Prepare for IELTS: Skills and Strategies focuses on the language skills and strategies candidates need in order to complete the four modules of the IELTS test. It aims to consolidate the skills required to perform well in the test and to familiarise the user with specific question types of the test. This book should be used with the companion titles **Prepare for IELTS: Academic Practice Tests** or **Prepare for IELTS: General Training Practice Tests** which contain sample tests.

Prepare for IELTS: Skills and Strategies is in two volumes: **Book One – Listening and Speaking**, and **Book Two – Reading and Writing**. Topics, skills and strategies studied in one volume are generic and complement those studied in the other, thereby enhancing your overall preparation for all four modules of the test.

Each module begins with a detailed description of the contents and format of each test. All question types are covered and practice opportunities given. Strategies are emphasised and developed across all modules, using a broad range of topics appropriate for all sections of IELTS. All modules include **Reports** for giving feedback or as a checklist. For Listening and Reading, these Reports cover all question types and skills, while the Reports for Speaking and Writing address the assessment criteria and their constituents or sub-skills for these tests. All sections of each book have **Photocopiable Materials**, including Answer Sheets for Listening and Reading. Photocopiable Materials are identified by the icon .

All skills and strategies are further supported on-line with CALL (Computer Assisted Language Learning) **Tasks**, drawn from the INSEARCH Australia Network program **Study English: IELTS Preparation**, **Series 1** and **Series 2**, at www.australianetwork. com/studyenglish. These materials are identified by the icon .

The **Listening Module** includes an extensive range of listening tasks with transcripts and answers. Listening **Activities** are identified by the icon .

They not only provide practice in particular question types but also address general listening skills. **Practice Tasks** further develop language skills by focusing on numbers, distinguishing features and other key areas important to IELTS.

The **Speaking Module** addresses the three parts of the test and focuses on assessment criteria used to establish a band score for this skill area. Language functions are examined using a range of IELTS topics. Again there are **Practice Tasks** and **Activities**, supplemented with practice **Prompt Cards** for Part 2, and **Topic Cards** to give further practice in speaking (fluency and coherence) suitable for all three parts of the Speaking test. A **Speech Analysis Form** for pronunciation feedback is provided, as well as **Vocabulary Work Sheets** to organise and develop vocabulary and word forms by topic.

The **Reading Module** provides practice for all question types through **Activities** and **Practice Tasks** with appropriate texts for both Academic and General Training Modules provided.

The **Writing Module** addresses Task 1 and Task 2 for both Academic and General Training Modules, and includes **Activities**, **Practice Descriptions** (Academic Task 1), **Practice Letters** (General Training Task 1) and **Practice Writing** (Task 2). All assessment criteria are examined throughout this section, and sample essays include commentaries addressing these criteria. There is also a **Checklist** for Essay Writing, a **Writing Analysis Form**, **Practice Essay Topics**, and **Sample Essays**.

The skills you learn as you prepare for IELTS will stand you in good stead when you are working or studying in an English-speaking environment, but more importantly they will certainly prepare you well for IELTS, the test.
Good luck!

INTRODUCTION

ACADEMIC MODULE COURSE MAP

SKILLS AND STRATEGIES

GENERAL TRAINING MODULE COURSE MAP

"I try to listen to at least four or five
English speaking radio or
television programs each week.
I find this really helps me
speed up my comprehension"

UNIT ONE

LISTENING

LISTENING

ABOUT THE LISTENING TEST

Listening is the first module in the IELTS test, and takes 30 minutes. It consists of four sections of increasing difficulty, and there is a total of 40 questions to answer.

The test is played **ONCE** only. As you listen to each section you will be given time to read the questions, write your answers on the question paper, and then check them. At the end of Section 4 you will be given 10 minutes to transfer your answers to the Listening Answer Sheet. The Listening Test will last 40 minutes in total.

STRUCTURE OF THE TEST

The test consists of four sections.

Sections 1 and 2 are concerned with social situations and needs. These listening passages include:

▷ a conversation between two speakers talking about, for example, opening a bank account or asking directions, and

▷ a monologue about, for example, a tour of a museum or information on part-time English courses.

Sections 3 and 4 are concerned with study-related topics or mini-lectures or talks, with an educational or training focus. These include:

▷ a conversation between up to four people talking about, for example, a school project, and

▷ a monologue, where, for example, a lecturer is talking on a general academic topic.

You will hear a range of English accents and dialects, including Australian, British, North American, New Zealand, Irish and others.

> For information on IELTS and how to obtain the *IELTS Specimen Materials* go to **www.ielts.org**.

LISTENING

When listening we use several skills such as:

PREDICTING

Before listening, read the questions quickly and think about **who** is talking, **where** the speakers are and **what** is being talked about to predict the content.

RECOGNISING KEY WORDS

Identify **key words** in the question in preparation for the **focus** of your listening.

Key words provide the **main information** and are **stressed** by the speakers.

ANTICIPATING

Using key words in the question, **anticipate** (guess) the kind of information the task requires for a correct answer. **Think about** the word forms and tenses that might go in each gap.

Listen carefully for **signpost words** or **linking words** in anticipation of what comes next.

Listen for **repetition** in anticipation of information being confirmed.

LISTENING FOR SPECIFIC INFORMATION

Listening for factual information such as **numbers**, **dates**, **names** and **letters** (spelling) is an important skill requiring **accuracy**.

Listen carefully for differences in meaning, and words which are similar (synonyms) but slightly different in meaning.

Be aware of the different ways of saying numbers in **different situations**.

IDENTIFYING DETAILS

Before listening for visual details, think about the **vocabulary** that would describe any pictures, graphs or objects used in the questions.

When listening for details being described in pictures, graphs or objects, it is important to focus on **distinguishing features**.

LISTENING

LISTENING

→ **ACTIVITY 1**

Read Questions 1-9 quickly to predict the content. Identify the key words and anticipate what words are likely to go in each gap.

 Listen to the conversation about the Listening Test and complete the sentences in Questions 1-9 with a word or phrase.

EXAMPLE

The test is _____ 30 min _____ long and contains _40_ questions.

Suggestions for the gaps:
The test is **number and word concerned with time** long and contains **number** questions.

Sample Answer
The test is 30 minutes long and contains 40 questions.

1 There are _____ sections.

2 One section might be divided into several short parts of _____ minutes, or it could be one topic which goes on for _____ .

3 You have _____ seconds to read over the questions, and _____ to check your answers. You have to listen carefully because _____ .

4 One example of a 'survival situation' is _____ .
One example of an 'academic situation' is _____ .

5 Accents heard in the test could be _____ or _____ or _____ .

6   A monologue is _____ .
       A dialogue is _____ .

7   Types of questions include _____ .

8   You cannot always copy down the exact words you hear but you must show that you understand the _____ of what you hear.

9   You have to transfer your answers to the _____ .

> **TIP!**
>
> In the IELTS Listening Test you must complete the answers as you listen. You should try to do this when practising. Later, go back and listen as often as you like.

→ **ACTIVITY 2**

Look at the **Passenger Survey** form on the next page and identify the key words.

Ask yourself
▷ Do you need to write numbers or words?
▷ Try to anticipate what you think they will say.

Predict the content:
Who is talking?
Where are the speakers?
What is the topic?

Allow about 30 seconds to look at the survey.

Listen to the interview and fill in the survey form while you listen.

Passenger Survey

1 Date: *15 may , Thursday*   Bus Route: 440

2 How often does the passenger travel on this route?
Tick ✓ the correct box.

☐ less than once a month   ☐ daily
☑ twice a day   ☐ more than twice a day

3 Purpose of the journey. Tick ✓ the correct box.
☑ work   ☐ recreation
☐ education   ☐ other

How do you rate the bus service? Tick ✓ the appropriate box.

	1 Very Bad	2 Bad	3 Good	4 Very Good
4 punctuality	☐	☐	☑	☐
5 comfort	☐	☑	☐	☐
6 cost	☐	☐	☑	☐
7 cleanliness of the bus	☐	☑	☐	☐
8 service from the staff	☐	☐	☐	☑

LISTENING

The listening situations used in the IELTS test will be on general topics.

Sections One and Two are concerned with social situations. First you will hear a conversation between two speakers and then in Section Two a monologue about a non-academic topic.

Sections Three and Four are concerned with study or training. You will hear a conversation with up to four people (Section Three) and then a short monologue (such as a lecture or talk) in Section Four.

TIP!

Learn to distinguish between voices in a conversation – how many different speakers can you hear?

PRACTICE TASK 1

Use the following example to practise the kind of vocabulary and grammatical structures you might need in a social situation.

BRAINSTORM

Arranging to meet a friend

Asking for directions

At the shopping mall

Losing your wallet

Exchanging an item in a shop

EXAMPLE

Think about:

▷ What directions would you give to a friend who was meeting you at the shopping mall?

▷ What would you say to the security guard if you lost your wallet? How would you describe the contents?

▷ How would you ask directions to specific shops or to a bank machine (also known as a cash machine, Automatic Teller Machine or ATM) at the shopping mall?

▷ What kind of vocabulary and grammatical structures would you use if you wanted to exchange something you had already bought?

LISTENING

7

PRACTICE TASK 2

Look at the following four social situations. Use the key words to help you think about these places and the kinds of conversations you might have.

 BRAINSTORM

1

> In the library

loans or circulation desk, study areas, closed reserve, lockers, photocopier

> **TIP!**
>
> Try to increase your vocabulary around topic headings such as these. The more vocabulary you can use effectively and appropriately, the more likely you are to demonstrate your level of language development, and vocabulary range.

2

> At the airport

check-in, baggage, immigration, departure lounge, gate number, customs

3

> In a tutorial

preparation, readings, tutorial paper, summary, presentation, discussion, group work

4

> Looking for new accommodation

rent, lease, fully-furnished, built-ins, carpets, curtains, blinds

LISTENING

ACTIVITY 3

It is important to listen carefully to word endings. Practising saying pairs of words aloud will help you distinguish between similar or critical sounds, and to differentiate meaning.

Listen carefully for verbs which end in "ed" – the final sound could be pronounced as /t/, /d/ or /ɪd/.

> How would you say the following words?
>
> | work | → | worked | | stop | → | stopped |
> |---|---|---|---|---|---|---|
> | point | → | pointed | | thank | → | thanked |
> | move | → | moved | | attract | → | attracted |
> | visit | → | visited | | laugh | → | laughed |
> | bore | → | bored | | wish | → | wished |
> | want | → | wanted | | hate | → | hated |
> | dance | → | danced | | mend | → | mended |
> | love | → | loved | | | | |

> Practise saying the following words. Be careful to pronounce final consonants clearly as they differentiate meaning.
>
> | wash | → | watch | | wish | → | which |
> |---|---|---|---|---|---|---|
> | think | → | thing | | sum | → | sun |
> | dead | → | death | | face | → | phase |

Clearly pronouncing final syllables, and especially final sounds, is important when saying numbers.

Numbers ending in **–teen** and **–ty** must be pronounced clearly and distinctly.

> Practise saying the following, until you can distinguish the numbers clearly and fluently.
>
> | 60/16 | 50/15 | 40/14 | 30/13 |
> |---|---|---|---|
> | 90/19 | 80/18 | 70/17 | 1990/1919 |
> | 1880/1818 | 1770/1717 | 1660/1616 | 1550/1515 |

CALL TASK
www.australianetwork.com/studyenglish
Study English Series 1, Episode 25

LISTENING

There are differences in the way numbers are said in British (and Australian) and North American English. The British (and Australian) will often say 'double' when a number occurs twice or 'triple' when it occurs three times.

> Thus the number **973 1277** could be said:
>
> nine seven three one two double seven (British and Australian English) or
>
> nine seven three one two seven seven (North American English)
>
> ✓ Both are correct.
>
> The number **5999 1277** could be said:
>
> Five triple nine one two double seven (British and Australian English) or
>
> Five nine nine nine one two seven seven (North American English).
>
> ✓ Both are correct

The figure zero is often spoken as 'O' (oh) – except in decimals when it is spoken as 'zero'.

You need to be able to recognise various ways of saying numbers.

For example: 0.25 (nought point two five) could also be ¼ (one quarter) or 25%.

 ## ACTIVITY 3.1

Can you think of another way to say the following numbers?
Write them down.

1   three-quarters   _____

2   three-fifths   _____

3   May 3rd   _____

4   0.05   _____

5   ½   _____

6   three-thirty   _____

In what other situations do you hear numbers?

Can you remember your telephone number, PIN codes, student number or login numbers? Practise saying these numbers.

ACTIVITY 4

You will hear 10 sets of three words. Circle the word you hear twice. .

EXAMPLE

If you hear "18, 80, 18" you will circle "18".

(18)   80

1   (15)   50

2   bend   (bent)

3   (led)   let

4   word   (work)

5   16   (60)

6   (dish)   ditch

7   (bed)   bet

8   (13)   30

9   (seal)   seam

10 (slim)   slip

Numbers occur in many different situations:

▷ time, dates

▷ addresses, distances, weights, measures, telephone numbers, sports scores

▷ prices, costs, currencies, stock markets, percentages

▷ weather, temperatures, rainfall, tides

▷ ID numbers, PINs, passport and visa numbers, tax file numbers, accounts, codes.

ACTIVITY 5

You will hear ten numbers in ten short conversations. Write these numbers down as you hear them.

1 _____   6 _____

2 _____   7 _____

3 _____   8 _____

4 _____   9 _____

5 _____   10 _____

Dates may be written as:

▷ day/month/year in numbers e.g. 3/5/99 (in Australia and the UK)

▷ day/month/year in numbers and words e.g. 3 May 1999 or 3rd May 1999 (we say the 'third' of May, but don't write the abbreviation)

▷ month/day/year in numbers e.g. 5/3/99 (in North America)

▷ month/day/year in words and numbers e.g. May 3 1999.

If you do not have all three pieces of information you may use numbers, or numbers and words combined:

▷ day/month in numbers e.g. 3/5

▷ day/month in numbers and words e.g. 3 May or 3rd May

▷ month/day in numbers e.g. 5/3

▷ month/day in words and numbers e.g. May 3

▷ month/year in numbers e.g. 3 1999

▷ month/year in words and numbers e.g. March 1999

You may abbreviate the months, but use the conventional abbreviation such as Jan., Feb., Oct., etc. These can be found in a dictionary.

Do not alternate between day/month/year and month/day/year. Choose the way of writing dates which is used in the place or country where you are learning English.

TIP!

Be consistent. If you write a date one way, the British way, then use the same way the next time you write a date.

What is your date of birth? _____

When were your parents born? _____

When is your IELTS exam? _____

In spoken English we say :

Anna was born on the twentieth of April, nineteen sixty two. (British and Australian English)

Anna was born on April twentieth, nineteen sixty two. (North American English)

A **decade** can be written '1990s' or '1990's'. In spoken English, a decade may be referred to as 'the nineties' or 'the eighties'.

> **In which decade were your grandparents born?** _____
>
> **What decade did you finish school?** _____

A **century** can be written with a 'C' and a number (C21) or as an ordinal number (21st century).

Remember for temperatures (32°C), the "C" stands for either celsius or centigrade.

Think of some important dates in your country's history.
Write down which century the following occurred in.

EXAMPLE

> **A revolution or war** _____
>
> **A dynasty/monarchy/presidency** _____
>
> **A national hero/writer/poet lived or died** _____

The **time of day** can be written 'am' (abbreviation of Latin, ante meridiem) for morning and 'pm' (abbreviation of Latin, post meridiem) for any time after noon.

For timetables and itineraries, the time can also be written as 24 hour time using the 24 hour clock, e.g. 15.30.

Intonation is also important when we give numbers. Try saying the following telephone numbers. Notice that your voice should go up after each group then go down when you complete the whole number.

9599 3610   612 8853 2167   014 3888 5112   110 399 254

LISTENING

ACTIVITY 6

You will hear ten dates in these conversations. Write these dates down as you hear them.

1 _____

2 _____

3 _____

4 _____

5 _____

6 _____

7 _____

8 _____

9 _____

10 _____

CALL TASK
www.australianetwork.com/studyenglish
Study English Series 1, Episode 22

LISTENING

In English, **fractions** are often written as numbers but spoken with the first number as a cardinal number (a whole number: 1,2,3,4,5 ...) followed by the second number as an ordinal (the form expressing order first, second, third, fourth ...). For example, 2/5 is spoken as 'two-fifths'.

→ ## ACTIVITY 6.1

How would you say these fractions?

1/3   3/4   1/2   1/4   5/8   7/5

Halves and quarters are also used in fractions, percentages and money.

> Three-quarters of the students came from China.
>
> He only got three-and-a-half per cent interest on the investment.
>
> He won a quarter of a million dollars in the lottery.

When you understand the pattern you can express any fraction.

For Example:

5/15   (five-fifteenths)

7/8   (seven-eighths)

4/9   (four-ninths)

1/10   (one-tenth)

12/20 (twelve-twentieths)

Practise saying these fractions.

Percentages are written using the symbol '%'.

→ **ACTIVITY 6.2**

> How would you say the following percentages?
>
> 100%   2%   20%   5.5%   10%   110%

EXAMPLE

The word **percentage** is also used to suggest amounts.

> A large percentage of students travel abroad to study.
> A small percentage of those interviewed thought the test was difficult.

Decimals are written with a point, not a comma. When you say the numbers after the decimal point, you say each separately as individual numbers. So 25.72 would be spoken as twenty-five point seven two.

→ **ACTIVITY 6.3**

> How would you say the following numbers?
>
> 0.5   71.95   48.16   3046.20   9652.44   .25   93.5

You may also hear postcodes (area codes, or zip codes as they are known in the USA). Postcodes are written differently in the UK, Australia and Canada (and the USA). In the UK and Canada letters are also used.

→ **ACTIVITY 6.4**

> How would you say the following post codes?
>
> | SW 1 | 5097 | R2W 0M5 |
> |------|------|---------|
> | W 9 | HARTSW 95 | 2088 |
> | 200072 | CA 3051 | 3001 |

In the Listening section you may hear money referred to in British pounds (£) or dollars ($).

What other currency symbols do you know?

→ ## ACTIVITY 6.5

Match the currency with the country.

RMB (¥ – yuan)	India
EUR (€ – euro)	Great Britain
JPY (¥ – yen)	The United States
AUD ($)	China
USD ($)	The European Union
GBP (£)	Saudi Arabia
INR (rupee)	Japan
SAR (riyal)	Australia

NOTE

AUD is spoken as the "Australian dollar".

USD is spoken as the "United States dollar" or "greenback" (informal).

GBP is spoken as the "British pound" or the "pound sterling".

Practise saying the following currencies:

JPY	Japanese yen
EUR	The euro
RMB	Chinese renminbi
INR	Indian rupees
SAR	Saudi riyals

LISTENING

In Russia, the name of the currency is the "rouble" (RUB).

The French franc and the German Deutschmark are not heard much since these currencies were replaced by the euro.

ACTIVITY 7

You will hear ten amounts in ten short conversations. Write the amounts down as you hear them.

1 _____   6 _____

2 _____   7 _____

3 _____   8 _____

4 _____   9 _____

5 _____   10 _____

LISTENING

Sometimes the pronunciation of the letters of the **alphabet** can be confusing. The Americans pronounce the last letter of the alphabet 'zee', while the British, Australians and many other countries refer to it as 'zed'.

There are also differences in the way letters are said in British and North American English. The British will often say 'double' when a letter occurs twice. Thus, the word 'letter' could be spelt:

L-E-double T-E-R → British English

OR

L-E-T-T-E-R → American English

In the IELTS Listening Test you may be asked to listen to the spelling of a name and write the letters down quickly. Some common nouns or names in English, for example, the Engineering faculty, or Mr Smith, will not be spelt out for you. A student of English is expected to be able to understand these words/names and spell them correctly.

TIP!

Familiarise yourself with common names in English.

 ACTIVITY 8

Practise spelling aloud these names. Note that the pronunciation is often different from the spelling.

fountain	Houston
Belleville	Tasmania
Heathrow	laboratory
Eileen McCulsky	cafeteria
giraffe	Jeffrey

Be careful of the different pronunciation of 'g' /dʒi/ and 'j' /dʒeɪ/.

CALL TASK
www.australianetwork.com/studyenglish
Study English Series 1, Episode 9

PREPARE FOR IELTS: Skills and Strategies   INSEARCH ENGLISH

LISTENING

Skills and Strategies

ACTIVITY 9

You will hear ten names in ten short conversations. Write these names down as you hear them.

1 _____   6 _____

2 _____   7 _____

3 _____   8 _____

4 _____   9 _____

5 _____   10 _____

LISTENING

ACTIVITY 10

Questions which use visual information, such as charts, graphs, maps, plans, pictures or any other graphics, require the skill of identifying details.

Look at the following three graphs/charts.

Think about the vocabulary used to discuss this graphic information.

1   The first is a pie chart. What information does the graph show? Think of the language used to describe amounts. For example: a large amount, half, a quarter, two-thirds, the most, the least.

How would you describe the amount of toxic waste in graph A? Is it a large amount or a small amount? Does the amount vary in the four diagrams?

 Listen and identify the pie chart being discussed.

A

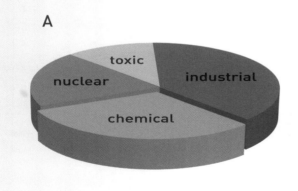

C

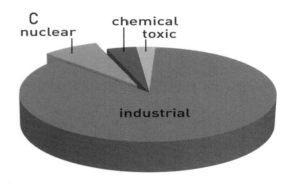

B

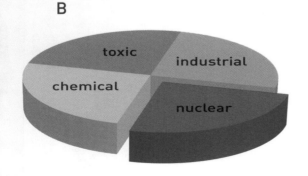

D

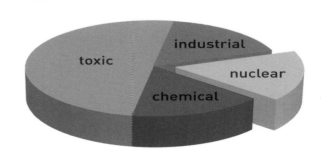

2 The second graph is a bar chart. We use these to show increases and decreases and to make comparisons. They are often measured in numbers or percentages and the terms horizontal and vertical axes are used. Look for the most significant differences.

10 🎧 Listen and identify the bar chart being discussed.

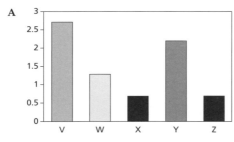

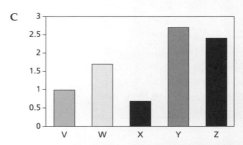

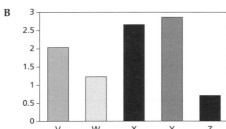

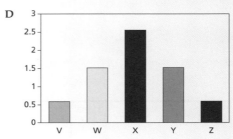

3 The third graph is a line graph. We use these to show changes over time and the rate of change. The horizontal axis often shows months or years and the vertical axis shows amounts, percentages or other data.

10 🎧 Listen and identify the line graph being discussed.

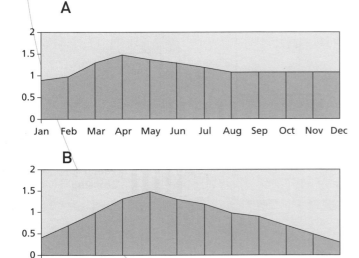

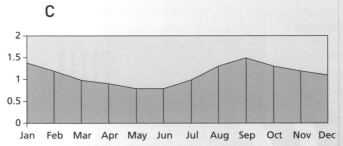

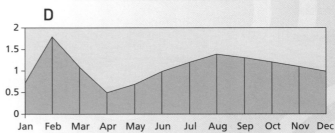

PRACTICE TASK 3

Look at the words in the box. These are used to explain location and to give directions.

go straight	when you reach the ...
opposite	turn right/left
on the left-hand side	on the other side of the ...
at the next corner	at the crossing, turn right
next to, beside the ...	

Look at the map below. Practise giving directions. How would you get to the post office from the bus stop? How would you give directions from the shopping mall to the library? How would you describe the location of the school?

If the map shows a compass diagram you may have to listen for directions involving the points of the compass, i.e. north, south, east or west.

TIP!

For questions in the IELTS Listening Test which involve directions and maps, listen carefully to where the speaker is standing. This is usually a point of reference in the listening.

Map of a small town

| Fire Station | Post Office | | Shopping Mall |

MARION LANE

PARK ROAD

LITTLE STREET

Hotel

Police Station

Library

GREEN STREET

School

Bus stop

Park

Hospital

Pedestrian Crossing

CALL TASK
www.australianetwork.com/studyenglish
Study English Series 1, Episode 20

LISTENING

When identifying details in a series of pictures, it is important to focus on distinguishing features. For example, what kind of vocabulary might you need to describe the physical characteristics of people?

Look at the pictures on page 26. What kind of information will you be listening for?

We usually describe a person's physical characteristics according to the following features: hairstyle, weight, clothing, complexion and height.

→ ## ACTIVITY 11

Put the following words under the appropriate headings in the table below.

plump, fairly tall, curly, casually dressed, quite formal, bald, slim, smallish, stylish, overweight, long, medium build, thin, average, spiky

HAIR	CLOTHING

HEIGHT	BODY SHAPE

Add more words you are familiar with in the table.

Which words would you use to describe yourself?

CALL TASK
www.australianetwork.com/studyenglish
Study English Series 1, Episode 23

→ **ACTIVITY 12**

Look at the following pictures of eight people. Can you match these adjectives to the people?

plump, fairly tall, curly hair, casually dressed, thinning hair, bald, clean-shaven, slim, a pleasant face, overweight, medium build, thin, average height, conservatively dressed

Look carefully at the following pictures and think about the vocabulary you might need in order to describe the physical characteristics of these people. Can you see any **similarities** or **differences** between these people? Can you **anticipate** what kind of information you will or might be listening for?

 12 Listen to the descriptions of the people labelled A-H in the illustrations below. Who are they talking about?

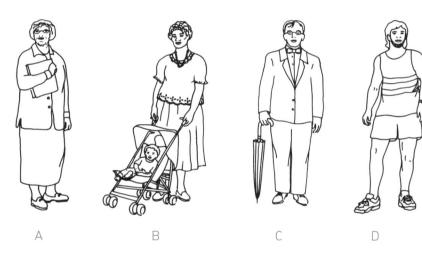

A   B   C   D

E   F   G   H

LISTENING

Listening for specific information is required when completing a form. The form will give you clues for what to listen for.

There are different ways to ask for information in English.

For example, forms often begin with a line like this:

Name: _____

To get this information, a questioner could say:

> **What's your name, please?**
> **Can I have your name?**
> **May I have your full name, please?**
> **I need your name. Family name first, please, then your given name.**

Think about occupation and education. Can you finish the following questions?

TIP!

Always try to anticipate the kinds of questions you might hear in a form completion listening task. Become familiar with the various ways that questions might be asked.

OCCUPATION

What do you _____ ?

Do you _____ ?

Have you ever _____ ?

EDUCATION

Did you finish _____ ?

Have you been to _____ ?

Do you have a _____ ?

TIP!

Key words help us to understand what a text is about. Always read through the questions quickly before you listen. Look for key words which will help you identify the topic and what kind of information to listen for.

ACTIVITY 13

Listen to the dialogue and fill out the application form while you listen.

Application Form

1 Family name:

2 Given name:

3 Nationality:

4 First language:

5 Number of years you have studied English. Tick ✔ the box:

Less than 1 ☐ **1** ☐ **2** ☐ **3** ☐ **4** ☐ **5** ☐ **6** ☐ **7** ☐ **more than 7** ☐

6 Level of education completed. Tick ✔ the correct box.

☐ Secondary up to 16 years ☐ Secondary 16-19 years
☐ Degree or diploma   ☐ Postgraduate

7 Date you wish to take the test:

8 Second choice of test date:

PREPARE FOR IELTS: Skills and Strategies INSEARCH ENGLISH

LISTENING

LISTENING

Listening for specific information requires listening carefully in order to differentiate meaning. This tests **accuracy**.

Look at these sentences. **What is the difference in meaning?**

▷ **Most** overseas students who want to study in the UK need to sit for an English test.

▷ **Many** overseas students who want to study in the UK need to sit for an English test.

▷ **All** overseas students who want to study in the UK need to sit for an English test.

The difference is in the **quantifiers** – words which show amounts. They are similar but each has a different meaning.

→ ## ACTIVITY 13.1

Look at the following groups of words. They are related but have different meanings. Check your dictionary. Can you use them correctly?

popular, famous, well-known

accident, mishap, disaster

hospital, doctor's surgery, medical clinic

Use the words above to complete the following sentences.

1 Tea is a _____ drink in many countries.

2 Tom Cruise is a _____ Hollywood actor.

3 Dickens is a _____ English novelist.

4 There was an _____ on the expressway this morning.

5 The new television series was a _____.

6 I felt ill last week so I visited the _____.

7 These days most women give birth in a _____.

You should also listen for the verb forms.

Look at these sentences. What is the difference in meaning? Which is the strongest statement? Which ones are the most polite?

▷ The students **may** be late today.

▷ The students **could** be late today.

▷ The students **will** be late today.

May, could, will, can, might, should, must, ought, would and shall are **Modal Verbs.**

Modal verbs are used when:

FUNCTION	MODAL VERB CHOICE
giving **permission**	Yes. You **may** leave now. We've finished the test.
describing **future possibilities**	It **might** rain tomorrow. **If** I get a good result, I **will** go to UTS.
giving **opinions**	I think he **should** do an MBA. I believe it **would** be a good investment.
making **suggestions**	We **could** go see a film or we **could** get a video and stay home.
giving **advice**	You **ought** to rest. You look tired. If you have such a high temperature you really **should** see a doctor immediately.
expressing **necessity** or **obligation**	You **must** stop work immediately.
expressing **ability**	Yes, of course I **can** swim! I **can** even do breaststroke and backstroke! When I was younger I **could** even do butterfly.

→ **ACTIVITY 13.2**

How are modal verbs used in the following sentences?

1 I **will** probably go to Tokyo next month.   Meaning: _____

2 You **should** take an umbrella. It might rain tonight.   Meaning: _____

3 In my view there **could** be two solutions to the problem.   Meaning: _____

4 I **must** hurry! I have a plane to catch.   Meaning: _____

Tense is also important. Look at the underlined verbs. Can you identify the tense?

▷ The school **will be** closed **next week.**

▷ The school **is** closed **now.**

▷ The school **was** closed in March **last year.**

Listen carefully for **Time Phrases** – for words like **now, tomorrow, yesterday** and other time phrases to help you recognise tense.

→ ## ACTIVITY 13.3

Match the following dates with the time expressions.

2015		this morning
2000		this evening
Nine o'clock today		a few years ago
Nine o'clock tonight		in the future

ACTIVITY 13.4

Look at the following time expressions. Would we use them to describe the past, present or future?

> the day before yesterday, now, in a fortnight, earlier today, later in the week, going to, ago, this evening, this weekend, last night, later that day, a few days later, after we finished, in 2003, during the year, after a few months, in a month's time, in the next decade, by the end of the year, earlier today, in a day's time, a week ago, last century, in the last 25 years, in the next decade, in a year's time, a few days ago, later in the year, in a minute, shortly, in a moment, the other day, right now

Place these expressions in the correct column in the table below.

PAST	PRESENT	FUTURE

CALL TASK
www.australianetwork.com/studyenglish
Study English Series 2, Episode 8

LISTENING

 ACTIVITY 14

Read the statements below quickly and **predict** the topic.

The speaker is explaining when different faculties at a university are moving to a new campus.

Identify the **key words** which will provide the focus of your listening. Do you understand their meaning?

 Listen to the passage and answer Questions 1–9 by marking T for True or F for False.

This activity tests the accuracy of your listening skills. However, the question type True/False is NOT in the IELTS Listening Test.

1	All Agricultural Science students will stay where they are.	**T / F**
2	History students will move to the new campus.	**T / F**
3	Some history teachers will move immediately to the new campus.	**T / F**
4	Engineering staff have already made their move.	**T / F**
5	The Philosophy department will move into the old Engineering building.	**T / F**
6	Part of the Faculty of Law is in its new premises.	**T / F**
7	The former law premises may become an art gallery.	**T / F**

LISTENING

BEFORE YOU LISTEN

▷ Read the questions and underline key words.

▷ Check where you have to write your answer and what form (a number, a name, a tick or how many words 1, 2, or 3?).

▷ Anticipate the words and phrases you will hear.

▷ Predict the content of what you will hear.

▷ Use the key words and any pictures or diagrams to help you understand.

▷ Anticipate synonyms and ideas expressed in different words.

WHILE YOU ARE LISTENING

▷ Listen to all the information before you mark your answer. Later information might force you to reconsider your choice.

▷ Listen for specific information.

▷ Listen for general information. Get the gist of the message and do not worry about every single word.

▷ Try to write an answer for every question even if you are not sure it's correct.

▷ Do not stop at an answer you do not know. Move on to the next question.

BEFORE AND AFTER

▷ At the end of each section, check your answers.

▷ At the beginning of each section, read carefully what you have to do. Try to identify unknown words and try to guess their pronunciation.

▷ At the end of the test, transfer your answers carefully to the Listening Answer Sheet.

PRACTICE TASK 4

You might have to listen for the distinguishing features (this means key or important features) of shapes, people, objects or plants.

This means looking at separate pictures and recognising how they are different.

Look at the pictures on the next page.

What differentiates one picture from another?

Think of the vocabulary you would need to describe each group of pictures.

Look at Question 1.

How are the shapes different?

Look at Question 4.

How are the hairstyles different?

ACTIVITY 15

 Listen and write A, B, C or D to indicate which picture is being discussed.

1
   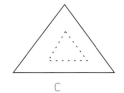
A   B   C   D

2

A   B   C   D

3

A   B   C   D

4

A   B   C   D

5

A   B   C   D

LISTENING

→ **ACTIVITY 16**

Pair with someone to do this activity.

One of you will be **Person A** and the other is **Person B**.
Look only at your own prompt card.

Take turns asking and anwering the questions.

PERSON **A** Which Room?

Ask your partner:

1 Where do I go to enrol?

2 Where can I find the Careers Adviser?

3 Where do I pay fees?

4 Is C130 the lecture room?

5 Which room is Medical Services?

Now your partner will ask you. These are your answers:

6 The Student Adviser is in Room D70.

7 Business Studies is in Room C19.

8 Photocopies can be made in Room 2 on the 3rd floor.

9 The professor's secretary is located on Level 16 in Room G90.

10 Library fines can be paid at the circulation desk located
on the ground floor.

PERSON **B** Which Room?

First, answer your partner:

1 Enrolments are in Room Q50.

2 The Careers Adviser is located in Room F9940.

3 Fees can be paid at the cashier in Room K33

4 No, the Lecture Room is J15.

5 Medical Services are located on Level 2 in Room V14.

Now, it is your turn to ask the questions.

6 Where can I find the Student Adviser?

7 Where do I enrol for Business Studies?

8 Where can I make a photocopy?

9 Where is the professor's secretary?

10 Where do I pay library fines?

→ ## ACTIVITY 17

Look at the **Swallow Life Insurance** form carefully and identify the key words.

Ask yourself:

▷ What kind of form is it?

▷ What kind of information is needed? Look at the key words.

▷ What questions do you think you will hear?

Use the following question words to form potential questions based on the key words.

▷ How ...?   ▷ Are ...?   ▷ Do you ...?   ▷ Have you ever ...?

Predict the content:

▷ Who is talking?

▷ Where are the speakers?

▷ What is the topic?

 17 Listen to the conversation and complete the details on the form:

Swallow Life Insurance

#				
1	Name of Applicant			
2	Address	*Strathfield*	Postcode	
	Age *35*	**3** Height	**4** Weight	
5	Marital Status	Single	Married	Divorced	Widowed

MEDICAL HISTORY

#				
6	Serious illness			
7	Major surgical operations			
8	Any current medical conditions			
9	Are applicant's parents still living?	Mother: Father:	Yes Yes	No No
10	If not, at what age did they die?	Mother: Father:	Cause of Death: Cause of Death:	
11	Is the applicant currently a smoker?	Yes	No	

LISTENING

PRACTICE TASK 5

Using these cue cards, work with a partner to practise having a conversation. Ask and answer questions that would allow you to complete further insurance application forms.

Role play the "Applicant" and the "Interviewer". The "Interviewer" has a blank application form, and the "Applicant" has the cue card.

Jennifer Evans, aged 27

Flat G8, 320 Victoria Road, Hong Kong
162 cms; 56 kilos. Single
No serious illness or medical conditions
Operation to repair damaged knee
from playing netball, four years ago
Both parents living
Smoker (1 packet a day)

William Lee, aged 45

2217 Macomb Street NW
Washington DC 20008
6 ft 1; 190 lbs. Married
Suffered malaria, aged 12
Has constant high blood pressure
Had operation to repair hand injured in
industrial accident in 1978
Father died aged 60, heart failure
Mother died aged 47, brain tumour

Elizabeth Nguyen, aged 36

552, 6th Avenue SE
Calgary, Alberta T2G 4S6 Canada
150 cms; 54 kilos. Married
Had pneumonia, 10 years ago
Takes medication since operation
Both parents deceased; father killed
at age 38; mother died 69, heart and
respiratory failure
Non-smoker

Michael Kim, aged 42

15 Rushmore Hill Road, Knockholt
Kent TN147NS
174 cms; 96 kilos. Married
Heart disease from childhood
Heart transplant, 1996
Medication daily for heart but fit
and healthy, gets lots of exercise
Both parents living
Non-smoker

Marilyn Habib, aged 55

Farm Road, Northland, Wellington 6005
162 cms; 60 kilos. Divorced
Operation on broken hip, 1999
Allergic to penicillin and to cats
Vegetarian
Asthmatic; takes asthma medication daily
Father died aged 40, industrial accident
Mother still living
Non-smoker

Scott Ivanisovic, aged 23

14 Philips Street, Shiftwich, 2678
180cms; 102 kilos. Single
Appendix removed at age 12
Broke leg playing rugby 5 years ago
Dislocated shoulder playing basketball
last year
Allergies, takes medication daily
Both parents living, however there is
a history of bowel cancer in the family
Non-smoker, enjoys a drink

LISTENING

Listening tasks will be easier if you can anticipate the key words you are likely to hear. **Key words** can be nouns, numbers, adjectives or verbs.

Look at the following vocabulary. Which words do you anticipate hearing in a report on earthquakes?

> tidal waves, disaster, destruction, volcanic ash, collapsed, flooding, rubble, epicentre, storm, earth tremors, famine, trapped, Richter scale, medical teams, emergency, explosions, fireballs, Fire Department, seismic research, evacuate, bomb attack, plane crash, nuclear disaster

ACTIVITY 18

Now listen to the report on an earthquake. Tick the above words if you hear them. Did you anticipate correctly?

Listen to the report again and answer the following questions.

1 **Where was the earthquake?**
  _____

2 **Which building collapsed?**
  _____

3 **How many people were killed?**
  _____

4 **How many people were injured?**
  _____

5 **What kind of rescue equipment was needed?**
  _____

6 **Where was the damage most severe?**
  _____

7 **How did medical teams reach the disaster?**
  _____

8 **How strong was the earthquake on the Richter scale?**
  _____

LISTENING

BRAINSTORM

Brainstorming is a good way to start increasing your topic-related vocabulary.

Imagine you are going to hear talks on **global warming**, **problems of developing countries** and **pollution**. What words would you expect to hear?

For example:

▷ Think about how climate change is affecting the region where you live.

▷ Think about how the growth in global trade has affected developing countries.

▷ Think about what measures your government might be taking to reduce pollution problems in your country.

Each of these topics will be looked at in succession. In the box below are some words for each of these topic areas.

Think about which topic they might relate to. Add them to the boxes below and on the following page for each topic.

environment	epidemics	toxic chemicals
floods	drought	lack of resources
CO_2 emissions	industrial waste	famines
globalisation	population growth	global warming
unemployment	melting icecaps	disease
	poverty	

EXAMPLE

TOPIC: GLOBAL WARMING

Add more words to these headings.

Adjectives	Nouns	Verbs
coastal	**environment**	damage
beachfront	**floods**	predict
predicted	**globalisation**	fall, rise, increase
natural	**drought**	cause
warm	**melting icecaps**	cover, immerse,
higher	**global warming**	drown
	damage	flood
	infrastructure	
	flooding	
	temperatures	
	rainfall	
	water	
	disaster	

LISTENING

→ ## ACTIVITY 19

TOPIC: PROBLEMS OF DEVELOPING COUNTRIES

Imagine you are going to hear a talk on problems in developing countries.

What words would you expect to hear?

Adjectives	Nouns	Verbs

TIP!

A good way to improve your vocabulary is by reading. Try newspapers, internet articles, *National Geographic* or magazines with general interest articles.

TOPIC: POLLUTION

Imagine you are going to hear a talk on pollution.

What words would you expect to hear?

Adjectives	Nouns	Verbs

LISTENING

→ **ACTIVITY 20**

How do you think this conversation could be completed?
Write possible continuations.

RESERVATIONS (dialogue)

Have you booked your **1** _____ ?

Why did you choose that?
3 _____ .

Was it very **5** _____ ?

I'm having a problem deciding between
7 _____ .

Yes, but the second one
8 _____ .

Yes I have. I am going to **2** _____ .

Oh, I guess the main reason was
4 _____ .

No, not terribly. It only cost **6** _____ .
What about you? Have you made up
your mind yet?

The first one sounds good.

CLUB MEMBERSHIP (monologue)

In this short talk I'd like to tell you about some of the future activities of the Club.
But first I'd like to explain the application procedures, because I know most of you
are keen to join.

1 To become a member of the Club, the first thing you must do is _____ .

2 Then, applications are accepted between _____ .

3 You must take your application to _____ .

4 In your application you must give us some details about _____ .

5 For example, you might like to describe _____ .

6 The cost of the membership is _____ .

7 There are only a few rules of the Club. I guess the most important thing is that
you must _____ .

8 If you have any problems with your application, you should _____ .

Well, now that application procedures are explained, let me tell you about
some of the exciting things we plan to do this year.

9 The first activity we have planned is _____ .

LISTENING

Here is another listening report on an earthquake but it gives more details.

Think of the effects an earthquake can have on a city.

Anticipate what the report might talk about.

Predict words you think are related to the following:

buildings	power supplies	roads and highways
houses	people	equipment

ACTIVITY 21

Now listen to Activity 21. Were your predictions correct?
Listen again and tick the words you hear.

☐ quake	☐ disaster	☐ epicentre
☐ wreckage	☐ rubble	☐ electricity cables
☐ rescue	☐ tremors	☐ trapped
☐ collapse	☐ fireballs	☐ minor tremors
☐ evacuate	☐ powerless	☐ Richter scale
☐ medical teams	☐ debris	☐ brought down
☐ emergency	☐ demolished	☐ explosions
☐ victims	☐ warning	☐ rescue machinery
☐ ruptured	☐ shortage	☐ brought under control

TIP!

IELTS tests your ability to understand synonyms. These are words which have a similar meaning. Widen your vocabulary and listen carefully for synonyms.

LISTENING

→ **ACTIVITY 21.1**

Which of the words on the previous page could be related to the following headings?

Buildings	
Power supplies	
People	
Emergency crews	
Roads and highways	

Often a news report will use synonyms.

Did you hear any synonyms for

debris? _____

collapse? _____

→ **ACTIVITY 21.2**

Put the words on the previous page under the correct headings.

Before (an earthquake)	
During	
After	

→ **ACTIVITY 21.3**

Use your prediction skills to suggest how the following two news segments might be completed.

Sydbourne earthquake

1 An earthquake measuring 6.5 on the Richter scale

_____ .

2 Emergency crews say that there is a shortage of

_____ .

3 A witness said that it was the worst

_____ .

4 The latest quake followed a

_____ .

 Now listen to the news broadcast and compare what you hear with what you predicted.

→ **ACTIVITY 21.4**

Storm lashes Sydney

1 Severe storms hit

_____ .

2 In the car park, a Toyota Corolla was badly damaged by

_____ .

3 Winds were recorded at speeds of

_____ .

4 In Lucas Heights, a tree fell on a

_____ .

LISTENING

A variety of task types are used in the IELTS Listening Test including the following:

▷ multiple choice

▷ short-answer questions

▷ sentence completion

▷ notes/form/table/summary/flow-chart/table completion

▷ form completion

▷ labelling a diagram/map/plan

▷ classification

▷ matching.

Practise these task types using the listening skills and strategies learnt.

CALL TASK
www.australianetwork.com/studyenglish
Study English Series 2, Episode 21

LISTENING

47

Multiple-choice questions

There are several strategies that can be used when answering multiple-choice questions.

▷ **Read** the questions in the time given and **predict** the content.

▷ **Anticipate** the vocabulary and ideas you might hear.

▷ Identify the **key words**.

▷ **Do not eliminate any answers** until you have heard the text, no matter how unlikely they may seem.

Part 4 of the Listening Test is a monologue – one person speaking. Listen carefully for intonation, word stress and rhythm. These speech patterns will help you to understand formal lectures and the important points the speaker is emphasising.

ACTIVITY 22

Listen to an introductory talk by a Student Information Officer and answer Questions 1-7.
Circle the correct answer.

1 **Overseas students will enrol on**

A 8th February
B 16th February
C 17th February
D 18th February

2 **Undergraduate students must enrol**

A between 8.00 and 10.30 am
B between 9.30 am and 12.30 pm
C between 12.30 and 2.30 pm
D between 2.00 and 4.30 pm

3 **The venue for enrolment is**

A in the Mathematics Faculty
B on Level 158
C in Room C658
D in Room C6

4   **At enrolment, all students**

A   must show a letter of acceptance from their faculty
B   need not show their letter of acceptance
C   need not bring any identification
D   must prove their level of English proficiency

5   **Students who have paid their fees**

A   should go to the International Students' Office
B   are guaranteed a place at university
C   must get a bank cheque
D   should pay a further $10,000

6   **The Student Card**

A   is issued before enrolment
B   has the student's identification number
C   is issued by the Library
D   is not laminated

7   **During university term, the Library will be open**

A   from 9.00 am to 4.00 pm
B   from 9.00 am to 9.00 pm
C   from 8.30 am to 9.00 pm
D   from 4.00 pm to 9.30 pm

LISTENING

Use the following strategies for questions requiring short answers.

▷ **Read** the question quickly and **predict** the content.

▷ **Anticipate** the kind of vocabulary you will hear.

▷ **Identify** the **key words**.

▷ **Do not try to answer from your own knowledge** before you have heard the listening passage.

→ **ACTIVITY 23**

Listen to the information about **London Heathrow Airport**. Write NO MORE THAN THREE WORDS for each answer.

1 Which terminal takes British Airways flights to Philadelphia?

_____

2 How long does it take to travel by coach between terminals?

_____

3 Where do you go if you do not have a boarding pass for a connecting flight?

_____

4 How many passengers can a taxi carry?

_____

5 How long is the journey on the underground?

_____

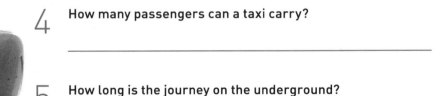

Sentence completion

Use these strategies to answer questions that require sentence completion.

▷ **Read** each partial sentence.

▷ **Anticipate** possible completions.

▷ **Look carefully at the words before the gap** – what word form is needed?

▷ **Be prepared** for synonyms.

▷ **Be prepared** for ideas, not just words.

Signpost language

Signpost words or transition signals (linking words) indicate the way a talk is structured and tell us when the speaker is moving to a new point in the talk. These words can indicate examples, additional information, similarities and differences, cause and effect, contrasts, or positive and negative points.

→ ACTIVITY 24

24 Listen to the Student Counsellor's Talk and complete the sentences below. Write NO MORE THAN THREE WORDS for each answer.

The counsellor's talk is about

students' problems

1   When they arrive, students initially feel

   _____

2   The first cause of student unhappiness mentioned is

   _____

3   The second cause of depression mentioned is

   _____

4   One cause of academic problems is

   _____

5   The counsellor advises students to be

   _____

→ ACTIVITY 24.1

24 Now listen again. Tick the following signpost words as you hear them.

☐ I'd like to talk to you about   ☐ Firstly

☐ In the first place   ☐ The second factor

☐ In fact   ☐ So

LISTENING

Use these strategies to answer diagram completion questions.

▷ **Examine** the diagram closely in the time given.

▷ **Predict** what the parts/sections/places might be called.

▷ **Anticipate** how locations/features might be described.

▷ **Listen** carefully to instructions.

ACTIVITY 25

Listen to the guided tour commentary and label the places marked. Choose from the box below. Write the appropriate letters A to J on the diagram.

A Information desk	F Circulation desk
B Catalogues	G Newspapers
C Reference section	H Returns area
D Current magazines	I Restrooms
E Photocopying room	J Conference room

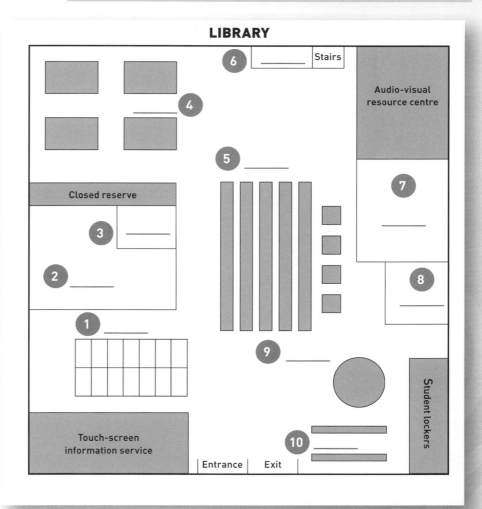

LISTENING

→ **ACTIVITY 25.1**

This extra activity tests your accuracy skills. However, the true/false question type is NOT an IELTS Listening Test question type.

 Listen again and mark the following statements true or false.

1 The tour begins at the loans desk.

2 The catalogues are not linked up to all the university libraries.

3 The library only holds English language newspapers.

4 Reference books may only be used in the library.

5 There are 15 colour photocopiers available for student use.

6 The copiers are coin operated.

7 Conference rooms are for small group meetings.

8 Inter-library loans can be organised at the loans desk.

9 Current newspapers and magazines are thrown away after a week.

TIP!

Information in the Listening Test is given in the same order as the questions.

Use the following strategies to help you answer questions that require form completion.

▷ **Read the form carefully** and think of how the words will sound when you hear them.

▷ **Try to predict** the answers but be careful. The given answer may be different to your prediction!

→ **ACTIVITY 26**

26 Complete the following application form. Write NO MORE THAN THREE WORDS AND/OR A NUMBER for each answer.

Starlight Video Shop
Membership Application

Name: (Mr) Mrs Ms Miss

First Name: **1** _____   Family Name: **2** _____

Address: **3** _____   Apartment: **4** _____

Houston, **5** _____   77042

Contact telephone numbers:

Home: **6** _____

Work: **7** _____

Date of Birth: **8** _____

I.D documents

Type: **9** _____

No: **10** _____

Password: *Horace*

Date of Application: September 9, 2006

Authorised by:

Labelling a diagram

Use the following strategies to answer questions that require labelling a diagram.

▷ **Look carefully** at the diagram.

▷ **Think about what you know** about the object in the diagram.

▷ **Anticipate** the vocabulary.

▷ **Predict** what to listen for.

▷ **Ask yourself** if there is a process or sequence of events illustrated?

ACTIVITY 27

27 🎧 Listen to the audio and label the parts of the bicycle pump and tyre valve. Write NO MORE THAN THREE WORDS for each answer.

THE BICYCLE PUMP AND TYRE VALVE

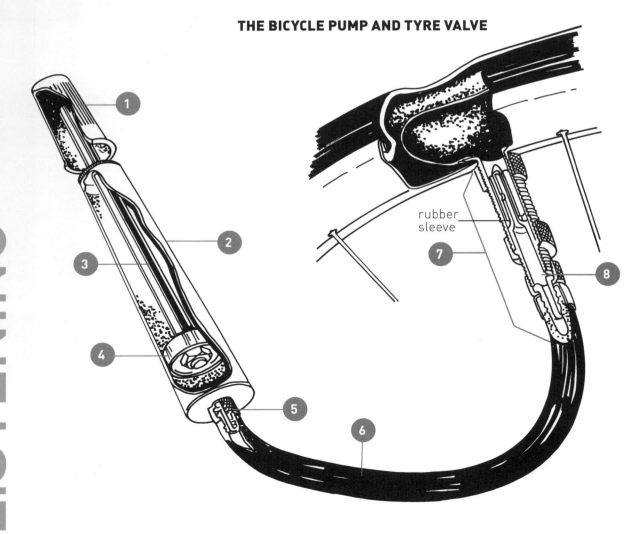

rubber sleeve

LISTENING

Use the following strategies to help you answer classification type questions.

▷ **Look carefully** at the key as it gives important information related to the answers. The items in the key may bear a direct relationship to the words they represent. For example, it may be the first letter of the word.

▷ **Identify** the **key words** on the horizontal and vertical axes of the table, chart etc.

 ACTIVITY 28

28 You will hear a talk about book sales in the University Book Stores.

As you listen, answer questions 1 - 6 by completing the table showing the type of books sold in greatest numbers at the different university book stores.

T Technical books

G General interest books

BOOK SALES

	Humanties Building	Engineering Building	School of Nursing	Sports Centre
1997	G	1	2	3 G
1998	4	G	5	6

LISTENING

Use the following strategies to help you answer matching type questions.

▷ **Look carefully at the pictures** in the time given.

▷ **Think about what you know** about the object in the diagram.

▷ **Anticipate** the vocabulary and ideas you might hear.

▷ **Identify** the **differences** between the pictures.

→ **ACTIVITY 29**

29 Listen and write A, B, C or D to indicate the illustration being discussed.

1

  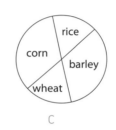 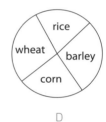

    A   B   C   D

2

    A   B   C   D

3

    A   B   C   D

LISTENING

Listening Answer Sheet

Transfer your answers from the Listening question pages to this Answer Sheet at the end of the Listening activities. In the real IELTS Listening Test you will be given 10 minutes to transfer your answers. Use one Answer Sheet for each Listening activity and the Practice Listening Tests.

1		21	
2		22	
3		23	
4		24	
5		25	
6		26	
7		27	
8		28	
9		29	
10		30	
11		31	
12		32	
13		33	
14		34	
15		35	
16		36	
17		37	
18		38	
19		39	
20		40	

Listening Total:

MULTIPLE CHOICE

SENTENCE COMPLETION

LISTENING QUESTION TYPES

MULTIPLE CHOICE

TABLE COMPLETION

FORM

SUMMARY

MATCHING

FORM

DIAGRAM

CLASSIFICATION

FLOW CHART

LISTENING

Listening Skills Report

NAME: _____

LISTENING QUESTION TYPES	Assessment	Listening Skills • Specific information • Main ideas and supporting points • Understanding speaker's opinion	Comments
MULTIPLE CHOICE	1 2 3		
SHORT ANSWER	1 2 3		
SENTENCE COMPLETION	1 2 3		
FORM/SUMMARY/DIAGRAM/ FLOW CHART/TABLE COMPLETION	1 2 3		
CLASSIFICATION	1 2 3		
MATCHING	1 2 3		

1 = needs more attention   **2** = satisfactory   **3** = good

Suggestions

_____

_____

_____

_____

"My friends and I try to speak to each other in English as much as possible. Talking on the telephone is a real challenge—you can't use body language to help get your message across!"

UNIT TWO

UNIT TWO: SPEAKING

SPEAKING

ABOUT THE SPEAKING TEST

The Speaking Test is taken by both Academic and General Training candidates. It is a one-to-one interview of 11 to 14 minutes and is taken on the day of the examination or up to 7 days before or after the examination. The examiner is a qualified and experienced teacher, and a trained IELTS examiner. The interview is recorded for the purpose of re-marking if required, and also to monitor examiners.

There are three main parts to the interview and the examiner will guide you through these. In all parts of the Speaking Test the examiner will be in control.

PART ONE

In Part One, the examiner and candidate introduce themselves. Here you will be asked general questions on familiar topics such as your job, home and family life, your hobbies or interests, and other general or everyday topics.

You are required to give short answers in Part One.

Part One takes from four to five minutes.

PART TWO

In Part Two, also called the Individual Long Turn, the examiner will give you a task card with prompts and ask you to talk on a particular topic. You have one minute to prepare and you can make notes. You must speak for between one to two minutes. When you finish talking, the examiner may then ask one or two rounding-off questions to complete this part. Part Two takes three to four minutes including the one minute preparation.

PART THREE

In Part Three, the examiner will initiate a discussion of issues related to the theme of your talk in Part Two (the Individual Long Turn).

Longer answers are required in Part Three.

The discussion lasts between four to five minutes.

 TIME

Use a clock or your watch to time yourself when practising for the IELTS interview.

 NOTE

Remember: the examiner will control the Speaking Test, and will ensure that you do not speak for too long in any one section of the test.

For information on IELTS and how to obtain the *IELTS Specimen Materials* as well as the public version of the assessment criteria used for Speaking, go to **www.ielts.org**.

PREPARE FOR IELTS: Skills and Strategies INSEARCH ENGLISH

SPEAKING

ASSESSMENT CRITERIA

You will be expected to answer short questions, speak fluently and clearly on a chosen topic, and to interact with the examiner. The examiner will assess your English language level using four criteria, as listed below:

1 LEXICAL RESOURCE

refers to the range and accuracy of your vocabulary (correct words and word forms) and how well you express meaning and attitude. The examiner will also listen for your ability to circumlocute (find another way to express what you want to say, if you are not sure of the exact word).

2 GRAMMATICAL RANGE AND ACCURACY

refers to your ability to use grammar correctly. It involves the different tenses of English, subject/verb agreement, the length and complexity of sentences, the use of subordinate clauses and the range of sentence structures. Errors will be assessed in terms of how they affect your ability to communicate.

3 PRONUNCIATION

means how words and whole sentences are spoken. You are not expected to sound like a native speaker, but you should speak clearly. The examiner will assess the strain caused by the amount of speech which cannot be understood, and the extent to which your first language influences your pronunciation.

4 FLUENCY AND COHERENCE

Fluency is defined as speaking without too many pauses or hesitations at a normal conversational speed and talking with normal levels of continuity and pace. Coherence means how effectively ideas and language are linked and organised. This is achieved by using cohesive devices such as conjunctions, pronouns and connectors to ensure a logical sequence of ideas.

Based on each of these criteria the examiner will give you an overall band score from 1 to 9.

CALL TASK
www.australianetwork.com/studyenglish
Study English Series 1, Episode 8

SPEAKING

1 LEXICAL RESOURCE

The examiner will ask you questions about familiar topics. It is important you have a wide range of vocabulary on familiar topics and that you use the correct grammatical forms.

Vocabulary means several things:

▷ Choice of words for topic areas. You need a wide range of vocabulary for IELTS topics (refer to pages 87-88 for a list of topics).

▷ Ability to circumlocute, which means using your vocabulary resource to describe things when you might not know the exact or correct word required.

▷ Ability to change the form of the word according to use (noun, adjective, verb, adverb forms).

▷ Ability to adjust syllable stress according to word form (e.g. ˈ**in**dustry vs inˈ**dus**trial; ˈ**a**ccident vs acciˈ**den**tal).

▷ Understanding of appropriate level of formality in word choices (e.g. children vs kids; search vs look for; television vs TV).

SYNONYMS

We use synonyms for variety. Synonyms are words which have the same meaning.

For example, sport players could also be called team members, participants or sportspeople.

We can also rephrase words to explain our meaning (circumlocute).

For example: spectators; the people in the crowd; the people watching the game.

→ ## ACTIVITY 1

Look at the following words. Can you think of synonyms or other ways to say them? Check your dictionary if you are not sure.

leisure time	niece	snack food
apartment *	international student	suburb
sister-in-law	homemade	sports game

CALL TASK
www.australianetwork.com/studyenglish
Study English Series 2, Episode 2

NOTE

* Do not confuse apartment/ department/ compartment.

TIP!

Use the vocabulary sheets on pages 166-169 to build up your vocabulary and command of word forms, and to group your vocabulary by topic.

SPEAKING

One way to approach improving your vocabulary is to take a topic (such as food) and break it down as in the table below. Build up your vocabulary in a systematic way by adding words such as those in the second column.

TOPIC: FOOD

Meals	breakfast, brunch, lunch, dinner, supper, afternoon tea, coffee break, snack
Types of food	poultry (duck, goose, chicken – breast, legs, wings), beef (steak), pork (bacon), lamb (mutton, chops, cutlets), fish, vegetables, fruit
Cooking	fried, deep-fried, stirfried, roasted, baked, grilled, steamed, boiled, broiled
Vegetables	carrots, potatoes, beans, peas, pumpkin, broccoli, cabbage, lettuce
Fruit	oranges, apples, bananas, grapes, strawberries
Beverages	tea, coffee, water, soft drinks, alcohol (wine, beer, spirits)
Courses	entree, mains, soup, dessert
Tools	cutlery (knife, fork, spoon), china (plate, cup, saucer), glasses, pots, pans, oven, griller, gas jet, hot plate

After organising the subtopics and brainstorming words, try to think of some of the possible questions you could be asked on this topic.

For example:

▷ What is the staple food in your country – rice, wheat, bread or potatoes?

▷ What is your favourite meal – breakfast, lunch or dinner?

▷ What is the most important meal of the day?

▷ What do people in your country usually eat for breakfast?

▷ Is it better to eat alone or in a group?

▷ Is it important to eat healthy food? Why?

▷ Do you think people are eating better these days compared to 20 years ago?

▷ Is dieting a good idea?

▷ Is it advisable to skip meals?

SPEAKING

SPEAKING

Take another topic such as sport. You might also like to organise your vocabulary according to word forms, adjectives, nouns, verbs and adverbs.

TOPIC: SPORT

Adjectives	exciting, thrilling, fast, physical, professional, challenging, tiring
Nouns	teams, players, match, goals, a draw, World Cup Types of sports – football, rugby, soccer, tennis, polo, cricket People who play sport – footballer, swimmer, tennis player, golfer, cricketer, baseball player
Verbs	kick, run, score, cheer, shout, watch, penalise
Adverbs	quickly, accidentally, dangerously, vigorously, aggressively

Can you use some of this language to talk about why you think soccer (football) is popular?

 BRAINSTORM

Think what questions related to sport you could be asked.

For example:

▷ Is sport popular in your country?

▷ What is your favourite sport?

▷ Do you prefer to watch or play sport?

▷ Do you prefer to play an individual or group sport?

▷ Do any of the sports teams in your country compete internationally?

▷ Can people get too emotional or excited about their favourite team?

TIP!

Even if you are not interested in a subject you should be able to talk generally about it and use relevant and appropriate vocabulary.

CALL TASK
www.australianetwork.com/studyenglish
Study English Series 1, Episode 1

SPEAKING

2 GRAMMATICAL RANGE AND ACCURACY

The range of possible grammatical structures will increase as your language competence develops. The number of errors, or level of accuracy, should decrease at the same time.

Possible structures would include:

2.1 GRAMMAR CHOICES - STRUCTURES

STRUCTURES	EXAMPLES
Active and Passive	**Active:** I taught. **Passive:** I was taught.
Conditional	**Zero:** If it rains, it rains. I can't help it. **First:** If it rains, then I will ... **Second:** If it rained, then I would ...
Comparatives and Superlatives	Peter is taller than ... This car is more expensive than ... The more it rains, the more glossy the leaves become. Run faster, try harder. Run as fast as possible. He ran the fastest. He is the best.
Cause and Effect	Smoking cigarettes can cause lung cancer. Overindulging is the reason for weight gain. Because of the noise, I couldn't fall asleep.
Reporting	He said that ... I thought that ... It was stated that ... The report found that ... I saw/felt/dreamt that ...

2.2 GRAMMAR CHOICES – WORD LEVEL

Check your grammar and try to eliminate all errors.

CHECKLIST

GRAMMATICAL & LEXICAL FEATURES	EXAMPLES
Agreement	
1 Subject + Verb	1 I **am**/He **is**/You **are**
2 Direct object (after verb)	2 I tell **you**/You tell **me**
3 Indirect object (after preposition)	3 Give it **to him.**/Buy it **for them**.
4 Number (singular/plural)	4 One **child is**/two **children are** I **was**/you **were**
5 Gender (male/female)	5 lion/lioness, king/queen, he/she, his/her
Tense	
Present	Every night I **go** out.
Past	Last night I **went** out.
Future	Tomorrow night I **will go** out late.
Articles	
Indefinite	**A** man came into the room.
	He ate **an** apple.
Definite	**The** man sat down.
Zero	Apples are delicious in autumn. (No article).
Word Order	I gave a book to him.
	not
	I gave to him a book.

CALL TASK
www.australianetwork.com/studyenglish
Study English Series 1, Episode 13

Assessment Criteria

2.3 SENTENCE LEVEL

SENTENCE TYPES	EXAMPLES
Simple Sentence = **I**ndependent **C**lause (**IC**) Sentence = Subject + Verb	There are two writing modules.
IC + <u>Phrase</u>	There are two writing modules in <u>IELTS</u>. The test starts at <u>9:00 am</u>.
<u>Phrase</u> + IC	<u>In IELTS</u> there are two writing modules. <u>At 9:00 am</u> the test starts.
Compound Sentence = IC1 + IC2 Two Simple Sentences (i.e, IC) joined by a co-ordinating conjunction: • **F**or • **A**nd • **N**or • **B**ut • **O**r • **Y**et • **S**o	Prospective technical college candidates take the General Training module **and** prospective university candidates take the Academic one. There are two reading modules **but** all candidates do the same Listening Test. Candidates can take the General Training module **or** they can take the Academic module. Overseas applicants for universities need to sit the IELTS test, **so** many overseas students do preparation courses for this test.
Complex sentence A Comlex Sentence is a Simple Sentence (or IC) plus a Dependent Clause (DC). Type 1: IC + DC Type 2: DC + IC Dependent clauses are made by: **1 Subordinating conjunctions** (as, because, if, although, despite) **2 Relative pronouns** (who, which, that) **3 Participles** (present or past)	**1 Subordinating conjunction** Many overseas students do IELTS preparation courses **because** they plan to study in Australia. There are two different reading modules in the IELTS test, **although** all candidates do the same Listening Test. **Despite** feeling unwell and a little tired, the candidate received a Band 6.0 in the test. **2 Relative pronoun** The IELTS test, **which** is a test of four macro-skills, is used as an indicator of overseas students' English language proficiency. The student **who** arrived late for the interview was given a new time at the end of the day. **3 Participle** **Present participle** **Arriving** late for the interview, the candidate was given another time at the end of the schedule. **Past participle** **Having studied** for several months, the student finally received the IELTS band score he required.

SPEAKING

Relative or participial clauses can be reduced.

The IELTS test, (which is) **a test of four macro-skills**, is used as an indicator of overseas students' English language proficiency.

OR

The IELTS test, (which is) **used as an indicator of overseas students' English language proficiency**, is a test of four macro-skills.

(The last two sentences both use reduced relative clauses: without which/who, etc.)

After analysing the essay question, candidates should spend a few minutes brainstorming ideas for an answer.

(The first clause is a reduced adverbial clause; there is no subject or finite verb.)

3 PRONUNCIATION

Pronunciation means:

1 The sounds of English (there are 44 different sounds in English – vowels, diphthongs, semi-vowels and consonants, both voiced and unvoiced consonants).

2 Stress in words (syllable stress) and on words in a sentence (sentence stress).

3 Rhythm – stress patterns in sentences.

4 Intonation – voice inflection (rising or falling) across a message.

Problems in these four areas will affect how clear your speech is and therefore the ease or difficulty the examiner has understanding what you are saying. The closer your spoken language is to the sounds of English, the easier it will be for the examiner to understand you.

3. 1 THE SOUNDS OF ENGLISH

It is important to be sure that you are making the correct sound when you are speaking.

Example:	I'm hungry.	
	Would you like a snake?	snake = /sneɪk/
	Would you like a snack?	snack = /snæk/
	Was it **l**ight?	
	Was it **r**ight?	

It is important to distinguish vowels clearly, and also consonants.

NOTE

Relative or participial clauses can be reduced.

CALL TASK
www.australianetwork.com/studyenglish
Study English Series 2, Episode 23

SPEAKING

3.2 STRESS

Stress affects three aspects of a sound – the length, the volume and the pitch. Stressed sounds or words are easier to hear because they are **longer**, **louder** and **higher**, whereas unstressed sounds or words are shorter, softer and lower, and therefore not as easy to hear.

SYLLABLE STRESS

It is important for meaning that the correct syllable is stressed in a word, because stress affects meaning.

Stress is used to identify word forms:

Noun: 'import   **Verb:** im**'port**

Adjective: in**'dus**trial   **Noun: 'in**dustry   **Verb:** in**'dus**trialise

SENTENCE STRESS

Key words are stressed in a sentence. The stressed words are usually Adjectives, Nouns, Verbs and Adverbs – the bigger words!

'Paul 'went to a 'good 'school in 'Perth.

3.3 RHYTHM

Because stress affects the length of a sound or word, moving between a stressed and unstressed sound or word will have an effect on the rhythm of spoken language.

Rhythm in English is regular – like the beat of the heart, it is a pulse. Of course the pulse rate can speed up or slow down – we can speak slowly or quickly, as we choose.

Tapping out the regular rhythm of a sentence, the words in the sentence below can be placed easily under a beat.

1	2	3	4	5
'Paul	'went to a	'good	'school in	'Perth

Compare:

	1	2	3	4	5
Sentence 1	'Paul 1	'went to a 2 3 4	'good 5	'school in 6 7	'Perth [8] 8
Sentence 2	'Peter 1 2	'travelled to an 3 4 5 6	ex'cellent 7 8 9	uni'versity in 10 11 12 13 14 15	'Melbourne 16 17

CALL TASK
www.australianetwork.com/studyenglish
Study English Series 1, Episode 21

Sentence 1 about Paul contains 5 beats and 8 syllables.

Sentence 2 about Peter also contains 5 beats, but there are 17 syllables, more than twice as many as sentence 1. The beats are regular, and this means that all the extra syllables have to fit in between the beats. This becomes the rhythm of the language – the regular pulse of the stressed syllables and the rapid delivery of the unstressed syllables in between.

3.4 INTONATION

Intonation means the rise and fall of the voice when speaking. Moving from stressed to unstressed sounds will affect intonation, because stressed sounds are higher and unstressed sounds are lower. What's more, intonation patterns depend on whether the sentence is a question or a statement.

In English, falling intonation means certainty or a conclusion, whereas rising intonation means uncertainty or surprise. It is not quite so simple. Look at the table below. The greater the surprise, the sharper and higher the intonation.

FALLING INTONATION	RISING INTONATION
Questions – "wh" type: What's your name? Who are you? Where are you from?	Questions – Polar Interrogative type: Are you hungry? Do you work? Have you had enough to eat?
Statements or Answers Yes I have, thank you. It's cold today. Sydney is a beautiful city.	Choices on a list Would you like tea, coffee, orange juice ...?
Conclusions Last choice in a list Would you like tea or coffee?	Surprise He said what?!

CALL TASK
www.australianetwork.com/studyenglish
Study English Series 1, Episode 24

4 FLUENCY AND COHERENCE

Part Two and Part Three of the IELTS Speaking Test focus on the criteria of Fluency and Coherence. This is because in these parts of the test your answers will be longer.

In Part One of the test, short answers are expected. In a longer answer you have to think about how to organise your response. If you have problems with fluency, these will become apparent in this section.

Remember:

FLUENCY is speaking without too many pauses or hesitations, with normal levels of continuity, pace and effort, at a normal conversational speed.

COHERENCE means linking ideas and language together effectively and logically throughout the whole response. The examiner will listen for cohesive devices such as conjunctions, pronouns and connectors, and a logical sequence of ideas at the sentence level.

Coherence means both the logical organisation of information through the whole answer, using transition signals and other organisational language (pronouns, tenses, time words, appropriate conjunctions for cause and effect and so on). It also refers to word order, agreement of subject and verb, plural and gender agreement, pronouns and articles.

In the following sample answers, examples are given of the different ways coherence can be achieved in English.

Fluency is also assessed in pronunciation. You will need to monitor your own pronunciation including how smooth your speech is. Fluency refers to how many times you have to pause (umm ..., ahhh ...), how long these pauses are, how correct your rhythm and stress patterns are in English, and, as a result, how accurate your English sounds are.

Do you have a strong accent?

Do listeners sometimes have to struggle to understand you?

Are you often asked to repeat what you are trying to say?

CALL TASK
www.australianetwork.com/studyenglish
Study English Series 2, Episode 5

SPEAKING

There are several ways to organise your language to improve fluency and coherence, as listed below'.

1 Time order and tenses

2 Using pronouns

3 Using transition signals

4 Additional information

5 Contrast

6 Adding similar ideas

7 Giving examples

8 Giving cause, reason and result

9 Adding a conclusion

Following are activities to provide practice using these language choices.

NOTE

Understanding coherence will also assist you in developing your writing skills and confidence. (Refer to Unit Four, Writing pp 80–206)

1 TIME ORDER AND TENSES

Order words, such as first/firstly, second/secondly, then, next, last/lastly, final/finally, and so on, help tell the listener the correct sequence of actions.

→ **ACTIVITY 2**

Complete the following by inserting the correct time order word from the choices supplied in the box.

next	finally	second	first

To apply for a scholarship there are several things one has to do. Usually in the student handbook there is information on scholarships, so the **1** _____ step is to check the handbook. This information might also be available online, on the university web site. Then of course the **2** _____ thing to do is to get an application form (or again download one from the web site) and fill it in. Universities ask for letters of recommendation to support the application, so the **3** _____ stage is to ask two teachers to provide such a letter. There is sometimes a form to complete or criteria to address. **4** _____ , make sure you submit your completed application to the appropriate office or department of the university by the scholarship deadline.

SPEAKING

Choosing the correct tense and aspect (simple or progressive) and time words assists the listener in understanding the order of events in your response.

→ **ACTIVITY 3**

Complete the following by inserting the correct words from the choices supplied in the box.

in the end	just as	during	while
when	after	already	
had	was	before	

1 _____ I was driving along the Hume Highway to Canberra, my car broke down **2** _____ I was nearing Goulburn. I **3** _____ travelling with a friend. **4** _____ I went off in search of a telephone, we had tried our mobile phones but there was no signal. It **5** _____ been raining all the way, but luckily the rain had stopped and the sky was clearing. I started walking and **6** _____ a few minutes I found an emergency telephone on the side of the road. **7** _____ the time I was waiting, the clouds reappeared but **8** _____ it didn't rain. **9** _____ I got back to the car, the tow truck was **10** _____ on its way.

Assessment Criteria

2 USING PRONOUNS

Pronouns help track and follow participants in a text.

→ **ACTIVITY 4**

Complete the text below with words from the box.

themselves	them	he	his
they	they	their	
their	their	these	

Tutors have a really tough time these days. Tutorial sizes have increased dramatically, but the frequency and duration of classes has decreased. **1** _____ really are under a lot of pressure to carefully monitor all of **2** _____ students and to be available to help **3** _____ individually when needed. The problem for many of **4** _____ tutors, however, is being able to manage large classes individually with less time to spend with students. It's also often the case that many tutors are actually PhD students **5** _____ and are engaged in **6** _____ own research at the same time as teaching. **7** _____ obviously have a lot of responsibilities which are unique to **8** _____ profession. A friend of mine is a tutor in Japan, and **9** _____ has told me that the situation is similar there too. The good thing is that **10** _____ students are on the whole very motivated and independent.

3 USING TRANSITION SIGNALS

Sentences can be joined together and made more coherent using connector words. These are words used to give examples or explain reasons, to show time sequence or give extra information.

→ ## ACTIVITY 5

Fill in the blanks in the response below using the correct word chosen from the box.

although	moreover	not only	for example
so	also	however	firstly
secondly	but	in brief	

Australians really love the outdoors! **1** _____ , during summer many families spend their whole weekends at the beach or by the pool in their gardens. **2** _____ this, but the warm weather **3** _____ means that many choose to cook outside and **4** _____ BBQs are extremely popular in Australia and are very social events. This hot, mostly dry climate offers people an enjoyable outdoors lifestyle, **5** _____ it also brings several important health considerations . **6** _____ , Australians are more prone than other nationalities to suffering from skin cancers (melanomas) caused by too much sun exposure. **7** _____ , the tendency for people to regularly visit the beach and sit around outdoor swimming pools has meant that parents have had to be extra vigilant in teaching their children water safety and good swimming skills. **8** _____ , being outside exposes Australians to many varieties of wildlife such as snakes, spiders and sharks. **9** _____ , the danger of these creatures is usually exaggerated and it tends to be less serious annoyances such as mosquitos, flies and bluebottles (jelly fish found in the surf at beaches) that are the most irritating aspects of the outdoors in Australia. **10** _____ , the Australian outdoors offers lots of good times but also require's some very important health and safety considerations. **11** _____ danger lurks, most Australians really enjoy time spent outdoors.

→ **ACTIVITY 6**

Choose words from the box below to fill in the gaps. There are more words than you will need.

in addition	and	however	also
so	as	but	next

I've been living in Sydney for the last two years, **1** _____ I'm going to return to my home town at the end of the year.

2 _____ year, I hope to get a job in my country as a programmer. I realise, **3** _____ , it could be quite difficult **4** _____ there are many graduates who are **5** _____ looking for a similar job!

4 ADDITIONAL INFORMATION

 ## ACTIVITY 7

Read the following sample response and identify those words and phrases used to include additional information.

> Employers today are under more pressure than ever before to be flexible and responsive to their employees' needs. Furthermore, with the higher rates of staff movement, workers have now come to expect employers to offer them higher salaries, more career opportunities and greater degrees of autonomy. In addition, people are now able to work longer, and retire almost when they choose. As a result, managing this, on top of the day-to-day worries, can be very challenging for some employers, especially smaller businesses. However, in the long-term it can lead to a more productive workforce by allowing people to work who might not otherwise be able to (e.g. mothers returning to the workforce, or people with disabilities). Employers are able to utilise the skills and expertise of these people who can prove to be very loyal and efficient workers. What's more, companies that offer flexibility and rewards which are linked to high performance are also better able to recruit and retain the best employees. So, in the end, everyone wins.

5 CONTRAST

→ ## ACTIVITY 8

Complete the following by choosing the correct word or phrase from the box.

differences	different	but	similar
on the other hand	whereas	while	although

Driving a car in America is a very **1** _____ experience to driving a car in Australia. Americans drive on the right hand side of the road, **2** _____ Australians drive on the left. **3** _____ a lot of the road rules are **4** _____ , drivers can find the **5** _____ in measurement a bit tricky. Americans use "miles" to measure distance but Australians, **6** _____ , use "kilometres". Not only this, but Americans tend to use "gas" to power their cars, whereas Australians refer to this substance as "petrol". Even though American cars are usually bigger, there tends to be more cars in one family than in Australian families. Often, Australian families will share one car **7** _____ American families often have more than one large car. Having said this, Australian society is changing rapidly and in many ways is becoming similar to American culture. For example, the number of 4WD cars in families has risen dramatically in recent years. American cars are usually much larger than Australian cars and so now petrol consumption is quickly affecting attitudes to cars and driving in the US. **8** _____ Americans still worship their motor vehicles, they are now having to think carefully about how much they depend on them and what that dependence is costing.

CALL TASK
www.australianetwork.com/studyenglish
Study English Series 2, Episode 18

SPEAKING

6 ADDING SIMILAR IDEAS

→ ## ACTIVITY 9

Complete the following by choosing the correct word from the box.

both	similarity	either	similarly	similarities

Chinese and Japanese meals have a number of **(1)** _____.

For instance, both nationalities tend to have rice as the staple part of the main meal, and soup is also an important dish. Another

(2) _____ is Chinese and Japanese tend to share dishes

between diners, and **(3)** _____ drink tea with their meal.

(4) _____ use chopsticks. One difference is that the Japanese often sit on the floor and will also eat raw fish. Chinese rarely do

(5) _____.

7 GIVING EXAMPLES

→ ## ACTIVITY 10

Complete the following by choosing the correct words from the box.

for example	by way of illustration	an example	
a case in point	for instance	such as	in particular

(1) Because of urban sprawl many Australian native birds are under threat. The tawny frogmouth owl is _____ .

(2) Though it can be said that his work was influenced by the Beatles, it was John Lennon, _____ , who had the greatest influence on Simon.

(3) The recent rise in interest rates has affected the average Australian family. Let me, _____ , demonstrate with statistics.

(4) The abstract painting is _____ of Boyd's early works.

(5) There are many different ways householders can conserve water. _____ , invest in a water tank to collect rain water for use in the garden.

(6) Your Writing Task 2 essay is incomplete because it doesn't have any supporting sentences, _____ .

(7) The youngest group preferred outdoor activities _____ horseback riding, hang-gliding and snorkeling.

8 GIVING CAUSE, REASON AND RESULT

→ ### ACTIVITY 11

Complete the following by choosing the correct words from the box.

led to	as	flow	resultant
because	result	meant	means

In Australia, there are now many non-smoking areas in restaurants, bars and pubs. This is **1** _____ of the growing concern among Australians about deaths as a direct **2** _____ of smoking. Since the early 1990s, it has become increasingly less socially acceptable to smoke in public places, including restaurants and bars, and this has **3** _____ new laws and regulations which restrict smoking to small areas of public places. This has **4** _____ significant improvements in the environments of public places and hopefully improvements in public health will **5** _____ on in the future. For many people in Australia, this now **6** _____ a much more pleasant evening **7** _____ there is less smoke in the air. It is hoped that as it becomes more inconvenient for people to smoke, smoking-related illnesses such as throat and lung cancer and **8** _____ deaths will decline over time.

9 ADDING A CONCLUSION

In English there are several types of conclusions and thus there are several language choices. These include:

1 concluding remarks or comments.

2 conclusions to a process or procedure.

3 conclusions to an essay.

To introduce or signal concluding remarks we can say:

in other words	in short
in brief	in the end
indeed	

When **telling a story with a message or moral**, there are other less formal choices:

when all is said and done (informal)

at the end of the day (informal)

all in all

Well it takes all kinds, doesn't it?

When describing the stages in a **process or procedure**, where there is a sequence of actions or activities, Transition Signals or set phrases are used:

Adjectives	final, last
Adverbs	finally, lastly
Phrases	in/at the end, in conclusion, the last stage, the final step

To conclude an **essay** we can write:

in conclusion	in summary
to conclude	to sum up

→ **ACTIVITY 12** Match the sentence on the left with an appropriate conclusion in the right column.

1	To begin the process the letter is posted.	A	In brief, if you have enough money you can enjoy an exciting and refreshing few days in the snow fields.
2	Glass is produced from three basic materials – sand, limestone and soda ash.	B	At the end of the day, if you have a good degree you can expect to land a job with a top company.
3	Skiing can be an expensive but exhilarating sport.	C	In conclusion, the introduction of computers into offices and most businesses, both large and small has had an enormous impact on the efficient storage of information, as well as enabling organisations to sort and search for information quickly and easily.
4	Employers these days are looking for young graduates with marketable qualifications from key universities.	D	To sum up, enrolments in the IT diploma declined from Japan and Korea, but increased for the other two countries, while the number of students studying in the business diploma rose with record numbers enrolling from all four countries.
5	We went across Europe and visited about ten countries and hundreds of museums and churches in about four weeks.	E	In other words, before you go swimming at any beach along the Australian coast, make sure you are not alone, are a strong swimmer and that you take precaution from dangerous sea creatures.
6	Computers have been introduced into all offices and businesses and have made dramatic improvements in storing, organising and retrieving information.	F	Well it takes all kinds, doesn't it.
7	I must tell you - the new receptionist began work today and proved to be interested and motivated, but the accountant we've hired has turned out to be difficult and demanding.	G	The final stage is when bottles are formed and the mould is removed. The bottles are ready to be used.
8	Technology has changed the way we communicate, the way we study and the way we are entertained.	H	All in all it was a stimulating but busy and tiring holiday.
9	The graph presents data on enrolments in several diploma programs from four Asian countries, namely Japan, Korea, Singapore and Thailand.	I	Finally, after a day or so the letter is delivered to the destination.
10	Swimming in Australian waters can be quite dangerous, as tides and rips are strong and the waters are sometimes open to stinging jellyfish and man-eating sharks.	J	In summary, technology has had a significant and varied impact on our lives.

TOPICS FOR IELTS

The topics in the Speaking Test are familiar – family, society, education, habits, hobbies, employment, transport and so on.

These major topics can be broken down into subtopics, for example:

TIP!

It is important to predict possible topics and themes of the questions you might be asked. Preparation for the Writing Test will help you predict questions for the Speaking Test.
(See page 88 for possible IELTS topics.)

SOCIETY

- ceremonies; festivals; cultural events
- youth problems; ageing society
- age of consent; marriage and divorce; parenting*
- community services; organisation and planning for communities

FAMILY

- relationships; nuclear and extended family; large and small families
- roles and responsibilities in the family; children and parents; children and siblings; what we can learn from each other
- housework; sharing household chores
- sense of identity; love and affection

EDUCATION

- structure of education system; compulsory education; class sizes
- the modern classroom; technology in the classroom; learning styles; computer-based learning; competency-based learning
- cost of education; fees; on-going and continuous learning; learning for life; life skills; curriculum in schools
- the learning environment; punishment; role of examinations

TRANSPORT

- choices of transport; preferred transport; best form of transport; which is the safest/most dangerous form of transport; which is the most popular form of transport
- cost of public transport; should it be free; how to make public transport more popular

*Some IELTS topics sometimes overlap a couple of topic areas.

SPEAKING

When preparing for IELTS, it is a good idea to brainstorm major topic areas, and then aspects of these, or subtopics.

TOPICS	SUBTOPICS
Family	role of parents; marriage; children; family planning; age of consent; responsibilities of husbands and wives; duties around the house; nuclear or extended family; generation gap; managing children; family relationships; children's duties towards parents
Society	youth problems; ageing society; population control; traditional culture vs popular culture; Americanisation of world cultures; fashion; music; arts; festivals; holidays; vacations; urban planning
Education	teacher and student relations; technology in the classroom; punishment; examinations; role and place of computers; homework; uniforms; after-school activities; compulsory education; single-sex schools; on-going and continuous education; private versus public education; cost of education
Health	traditional and western medicines; alternative medicines; cost of health cover; diet and exercise; role of doctors
Transport	types of transport; cost of transport; comfort and public transport; driving, motor cars and roads; safety and danger
Commerce	shopping; fashions and fads; customer service; shopping online; internet shopping; all-night shopping
Communication	global; internet; access to information; privacy; good and bad communication
Media	role of the media; types of media; privacy and the media; news and reporting; role of reporters and journalists; censorship; control of the media
Employment	training; automation; employment conditions; workers' rights; team skills; on-going training; responsibility of the employer; holidays
Environment	pollution; tourism and the environment; global warming; saving water; alternate sources of energy; clean fuel; nuclear power; greenhouse effect; El Niño; role of the government; individual's responsibilities; recycling
Architecture	zoning; urban landscapes; environmentally friendly design; energy-saving design; importance of old buildings; cultural heritage
Sciences	biology; botany; astronomy; physics; geology; geography; mathematics; sociology; anthropology; psychology

LANGUAGE FUNCTIONS

The following key language functions are covered in all the parts of the Speaking Test.

It is important that you understand each of these language functions:

▷ providing personal and non-personal information

▷ describing people, places and employment

▷ expressing preferences, likes and dislikes

▷ giving reasons, explanations and examples

▷ describing an event

▷ expressing future plans, hopes and wishes

▷ speculating and predicting

▷ expressing enthusiasm

▷ comparing and contrasting

▷ expressing certainty and uncertainty

▷ expressing opinions

▷ expressing conditions

▷ making suggestions.

ASKING FOR REPETITION

If you don't understand a question or word in Parts 1 and 2 of the IELTS Speaking Test, you can ask the examiner to repeat the question but you can't ask for a different speaking topic!

The examiner can only repeat the question and cannot change it.

For example, you can use the following language choices:

> I'm sorry. I don't understand.
>
> Excuse me. I didn't hear what you said.
>
> Could you repeat the question please?
>
> Sorry. Could you say that again please?

It is possible to ask what a particular word means:

> I'm sorry. What does the word .... mean?

In Part 3, however, it **is** possible to ask for the question to be re-phrased.

SPEAKING

The functions listed below might occur in any section of the test and within any topic area.

TOPICS	FUNCTIONS
Personal	Providing personal and non-personal information/including expressing information numerically
Food	
Education	
Customs/traditions	Describing people and/or places (family, friends, family home)
Leisure	
Music/reading habits	Making comparisons
Sport	Describing preferences, likes/dislikes
Fashion	
Travel – holidays and vacations	Giving reasons/explanations, giving examples
Media	Justifying and supporting opinions
Technology	
Environment	Expressing future plans/hopes/wishes/dreams/desires
News/communication	
Health	Speculating about or predicting the future

In Part One (page 92) and Part Three (page 125), the questions the examiner asks imply certain language functions and oblige you to use these functions in your response.

For example:

TOPIC: TRAVEL

POSSIBLE QUESTIONS	LANGUAGE FUNCTION REQUIRED
1 Why do you think people like travelling?	Speculation
2 Why do you think so many people want to visit China?	Speculation
3 Do you think tourism is a well-developed industry in China?	Opinion
4 Which is better – to travel alone or with a group of friends?	Comparison
5 Which do you prefer – backpacking or travelling first class?	Preferences
6 Tell me about a recent short holiday you took.	Narration
7 Describe the most beautiful place you visited.	Description

SPEAKING

TOPIC: SPORT

POSSIBLE QUESTIONS	LANGUAGE FUNCTION REQUIRED
1 Based on present performance and past history, will Brazil win the next World Cup?	Prediction
2 Do more people watch sport than play it in your country?	Comparison
3 Why is exercise and a good diet important?	Explanation
4 Do you think playing sport can make people become too competitive?	Opinion
5 Why do people enjoy watching others play competitive sport?	Explanation
6 Which is more dangerous – football or basketball?	Comparison
7 Give some examples of dangerous sports.	Giving examples

Use the photocopiable sheets on pages 138 – 139 to brainstorm more possible questions by topic and language function.

PART ONE

The test begins with an introduction. In Part One of the Speaking Test, the examiner checks your identity and asks general questions about familiar topics. The different language functions require a command of certain grammar. Topics require particular vocabulary.

Function:
introducing yourself – providing personal and non-personal information including expressing information numerically

Grammar:
present simple tense; simple, compound and complex sentences

Vocabulary:
self, family, residence, employment, education, likes/dislikes, hobbies

→ **ACTIVITY 13**

Look at the following and complete the question by inserting a word or words that someone might ask when first meeting you.

1 What's your _____ ?
2 Do you _____ or are you _____ ?
3 What do you like about _____ ?
4 Where do you _____ ?
5 How long have you _____ ?

Here is one person's possible self-introduction.

Compound sentence

SAMPLE ANSWER ☞

"
1 My name is Phillip and I **come** from Paris. **2** At the moment I **am** a student, and **3** I **am studying** a full-time English program at INSEARCH. This is in preparation for studying an MBA at the University of Technology, Sydney. **4** I **arrived** in Sydney a couple of months ago and I **have been studying** English for 10 weeks. **5** I really **enjoy** learning English **6** because it's a global language and knowing it **gives** me access to a world of information and contacts. **7** I hope to get a job with a multinational company.
"

Simple sentence   **Complex sentence**

NOTE

Note verb tenses - simple past, simple present, present continuous and present perfect (highlighted in bold).

Note range of sentence types – simple, compound and complex.

Note numerical information – a couple of months ago, 10 weeks.

Such a long response would NOT be expected in Part One. This is actually the answer to several questions, a group or bracket of questions.

1 What's your name? Where are you from?

2 Do you work or are you a student?

3 What are you studying?

4 How long have you been studying this?

5 Do you like what you are studying?

6 Why?

7 What do you plan to do when you finish your studies?

Remember answers in Part One only need to be short.

Function:
describing people and/or places (family, friends, favourite teacher, family home, favourite room or place).

Grammar:

▷ simple present tense, present perfect tense, time phrases

▷ simple, compound and complex sentences

▷ prepositions of time and place

Vocabulary:
family, accommodation, rooms, places,

 BRAINSTORM

Think about the following topic: **Family**

Write the word **Family** in the middle of a blank sheet of paper. Then, think of as many words as you can which relate to this topic.

EXAMPLE

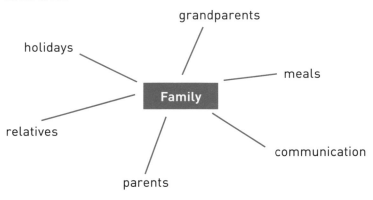

Think about how you might respond to the following questions:

1 Do you have a large or small family?

2 Do you have many relatives or extended family, for example, aunts, uncles, cousins, nephews, in-laws or stepbrothers and sisters?

3 How often do you see your family?

Here is one person's response to being asked about his/her family.

Simple sentences

Compound sentences

**SAMPLE
ANSWER**

NOTE

Note verb tenses – simple past, simple present, present continuous and present perfect (highlighted in bold).

Note range of sentence types – simple, compound and complex.

> I **live** at home with my parents. My father **is** a businessman and my mother **is** a housewife. I **have** an older brother but he **doesn't live** with us but instead **lives** with his new wife. He **is** a teacher. Also I **have** a younger sister who **is studying** in the States at the moment. She **is** quite intelligent and **is studying** for a PhD in Education.

Complex sentence

BRAINSTORM

Think about the following topic and potential questions:
the type of accommodation you live in.

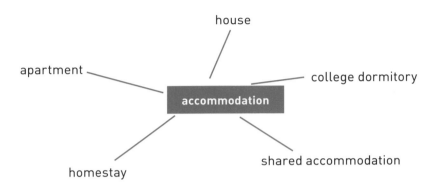

Think about how you might respond to the following questions:

Do you live in a house or an apartment?
Do you like where you live?
Are you sharing or living alone?
What are some of the problems with sharing?
Can you describe your accommodation?
Which is your favourite room?
Do you plan to live there for a long time? Why? Why not?

Here is one person's response to being asked about his/her current accommodation.

Simple sentences

 SAMPLE ANSWER

Compound sentence

> My apartment **is** very small but comfortable. It **has** a living room, a kitchen, a bedroom and a bathroom. At the entrance two doors **lead** into the bathroom and the bedroom. The bathroom **is** on the far left, and the bedroom **is** next to it. Directly in front of the entrance **is** the kitchen. Between the bedroom and the kitchen there **is** a large storage cupboard. On the right side of the entrance **is** the living room, which **is** quite large because it also **serves** as a dining room. It **has** a dining table which **seats** four people at one end of the room. Along the back wall of the living room **is** a built-in bookcase, and next to that **is** a door which **leads** to a narrow balcony.

Complex sentences

 NOTE

Note verb tenses (highlighted in bold).

Note range of sentence types.

Note prepositions and prepositional phrases (underlined).

Note vocabulary for rooms and furniture.

PREPOSITIONS OF PLACE

 ## ACTIVITY 14

Fill in the following description of an apartment layout by choosing the correct prepositions of place. Choose words from the list below.

under	off	onto	in	below
on	in	on	on	from
opposite	next	on	at	along

Actually I share a flat with a couple of other students. It is

1 _____ the third floor of a modern apartment

block **2** _____ the centre of the city, **3** _____

the corner of Pitt and Goulburn Streets. Some other students live

a few floors **4** _____ . It's a bit noisy and we can feel the

trains in the subway which is **5** _____ our building.

In our apartment there are three bedrooms, one with an ensuite

(that's mine!). When you enter the apartment the kitchen is

6 _____ the right. It opens **7** _____ the dining

room. You enter the living room **8** _____ the dining

room. **9** _____ the living room is a long balcony. There

is a hallway or corridor which runs **10** _____ past the

bedrooms, and **11** _____ the end of the hall is a cupboard.

The main bathroom is **12** _____ the kitchen, **13** _____

to the small study or computer room. There is a swimming pool,

gym and sauna **14** _____ the basement and a barbecue area

15 _____ the roof.

 NOTE

When describing places you will need to be able to use prepositions correctly.

Part One

 BRAINSTORM

Think about any specialist vocabulary you might need to describe your current job (or the job you might hope to have one day).

EMPLOYMENT

For example: computer programmer, geriatric nurse, graphic designer, sports manager, account manager.

Think about:

▷ What skills do you/will you use in your job?

▷ What do you hope to be doing in ten years' time?

▷ What subjects must you study, or what work experience do you need, to succeed in this type of job?

▷ What is the best thing about this job?

Here is one person's response to being asked about employment.

TIP!

Make sure you speak up and try to give more information than yes or no. In Part One, however, you only need to give short answers. Also don't forget to answer the specific question the examiner asks!

SAMPLE ANSWER

 NOTE

Note verb tenses (in bold).

Note range of sentence types.

Simple sentence

Complex sentence

> I **am** a sportswear designer for a large fashion label in Bangkok. I **use** a computer program to design garments although I still **prefer** to do some designs by hand using paper and pencil! I really **like** the creativity involved in my job, and I also **enjoy** the chance to learn new skills.

Complex sentence

CALL TASK
www.australianetwork.com/studyenglish
Study English Series 2, Episode 15

> **Function:**
> expressing preferences, likes and dislikes
>
> **Grammar:**
> simple present tense, modal verbs and range of sentence types
>
> **Vocabulary:**
> hobbies, interests, adjectives, quantifiers

 BRAINSTORM

Brainstorm possible questions or question areas.

▷ My ideal home.

▷ A perfect day.

▷ My favourite form of communication.

▷ What I like to do on my holidays (on vacation).

PRACTICE TASK

Read the following statements. Number them 1-4, where 1 means you strongly agree and 4 means you agree the least.

1	**2**	**3**	**4**
strongly agree	somewhat agree	slightly disagree	least agree

1 **My ideal home would be:**
___ a high-rise apartment block   ___ a house in the countryside
___ a cabin in the mountains   ___ a house in the city

2 **A perfect day is spent:**
___ playing sport   ___ in the shopping mall or markets
___ having lunch with friends   ___ outdoors at a beach or in a park

3 **My favourite form of communication is:**
___ mobile phone   ___ email
___ telephone   ___ writing letters

4 **On holidays I like to:**
___ relax on a beach   ___ be active and adventurous
___ visit cultural sites   ___ meet new people

Now choose one of the above statements and practise speaking on the topic. Give reasons for your opinions.

Part One

 SAMPLE ANSWER

Here is one person's response to being asked about holiday preferences:

> When I go on holiday I **like to visit** museums and historic sites as I'm really **interested in** history and I **think** these places can be **fascinating**. I had a really great time in China – the Great Wall and the Imperial Palace in Beijing were wonderful, and I'd like to explore other interesting countries in Asia. I'm not really interested in beaches or resorts – I **find** them **a bit boring** after a couple of days. Give me a museum and I am happy! I **prefer** historic places. They are **more stimulating**.

📋 **NOTE**

Verb tenses and range of sentence types.

Language for expressing likes and dislikes, interests, hobbies (in bold).

Language for making comparisons (for stating preferences).

The Great Wall of China

The Temple of Heaven

→ **ACTIVITY 15**

Read the following statements and circle the correct word from the choices in **bold**.

1   Sitting in lectures all day is extremely **tiring/tired**. When I get home at night I am really **tiring/tired**.

2   They can be **stimulating/stimulated** sometimes, and sometimes they can be **boring/bored**. I am really **boring/bored** in the accounting classes, but strangely I am **stimulating/stimulated** by finance.

3   For me, the most **fascinating/fascinated** subject is marketing. I have always been **fascinating/fascinated** by the big advertising companies and their strategies used to market a new product.

4   The most **embarrassing/embarrassed** time at university for me was when I arrived late for a tutorial, and when I sat down the tutor asked me a question and I hadn't prepared for it. I was so **embarrassing/embarrassed** I couldn't answer!

5   I am getting quite **frustrating/frustrated** trying to find the books for the essay in the library. The **frustrating/frustrated** thing is that all the books on the reading list have been borrowed and I think that they should be in closed reserve so everyone can use them.

Function: Expressing likes and dislikes

Language choice:

I love …   I really like …

I am really interested in … / I'm fascinated by …

What I really like is …

What really excites me is … / What interests me is …

I'm interested in …

I don't really like …

I am not really / particularly interested in

I think … is boring / I am completely bored by …

I dislike …   I hate …

Part One

To make what you say a little more interesting, it is important to support it with comments, reasons, explanations and specific examples.

TIP!

One way to make your response longer is to give reasons, explanations and examples.

Function:
giving reasons, explanations and examples.

SAMPLE ANSWER

Reason

Example

> I really like chicken dishes. My favourite is stir-fried chicken with noodles. We eat this a lot in my home country. It's simple to make but I like my mother's recipe the best <u>because she always uses fresh ingredients and lots of chilli!</u> We like it hot and spicy! I also like takeaway chicken nuggets which I often buy for lunch. I know they're not good for me but they are delicious and I can't stop eating them! Fast food, I mean American fast food, not Chinese takeaway, is becoming more popular because of the strong advertising campaigns, and I'm being influenced by it! That is, I'm not thinking about the nutritional value, so much as the availability.

Explanation or clarification

→ **ACTIVITY 16**

Fill in the blanks in the following sentences using the following words and phrases. Each choice can be used only once.

for example	for instance	such as
like	a case in point	an illustration
example	namely	

1   There are several interesting places to visit in London, ————— the Tower of London, the London Eye and the Houses of Parliament.

2   Fruit and vegetables are an important source of vitamins. ————— , oranges are rich in vitamin C, and carrots in vitamin A.

3   A lot of sports, ————— soccer, rugby and ice hockey arouse very strong feelings with the crowds who come to watch the games.

4   A recent game of soccer, a preliminary match leading to the World Cup, between two former national enemies is _____. Riots broke out around the city when the visiting country used aggressive tactics to win.

5   A good _____ of the warming of the Earth's atmosphere is the melting of glaciers in New Guinea. Another is the receding polar icecaps.

6   There are important differences between Asian and western meals. _____ , Asians share bowls of food, whereas at a western dining table, each person is given an individual serving.

7   There are two famous operas taken from Beaumarchais' plays, _____ Mozart's *'The Marriage of Figaro'* and Rossini's *'The Barber of Seville'*.

8   People's eating habits are changing. ————— of this is the rapid expansion of takeaway food outlets. Another is the increase in obesity.

Part One

> **Function:**
> describing an event.
>
> **Grammar:**
> ▷ simple present tense, modal verbs and range of sentence types
> ▷ adverbs of frequency
>
> **Vocabulary:**
> festivals, customs, traditions

TIP!

Combine all answers for a good long response which is ideal for Part Two and Three of the Speaking Test.

In Part One there will be a series of questions relating to one particular topic. Answer the questions posed by the examiner with short, interesting responses.

If you add all these short responses together, you will get a good long response! We will look at longer responses when dealing with Part Two and Part Three of the test, where longer answers are expected.

TOPIC: A SPECIAL DAY OR FESTIVAL

Question:
Describe a popular festival or holiday in your country.

SAMPLE ANSWER

> "
> The 14th February is referred to as St. (Saint) Valentine's Day and is the day which many countries now set aside for lovers, to remember the special person you love (girlfriend, boyfriend, husband, wife) and even friends.
> "

Question:
What is the origin of this day?

SAMPLE ANSWER

> This day was identified by the Romans and was a pagan festival about 2000 years ago. This ancient link is lost now and people, encouraged by commercial businesses such as restaurants, florists, chocolate shops and greeting card companies, simply take the opportunity to indulge their Valentine.

Question:
What do people do on this day?

SAMPLE ANSWER

> It is especially common with couples to give a bunch of flowers, usually red roses, a box of chocolates and have a romantic meal at a lovely and intimate restaurant, sipping a glass of champagne — French of course, because France is the country of romance!

Question:
Do you think people will continue to celebrate this day in 25 years' time?

SAMPLE ANSWER

> Yes, I do, because it is a happy and colourful day — and it is very romantic. In the world today there are not many opportunities to be romantic. Everyone is interested in romance, especially when they are involved! We have seen this particular day picked up by many countries around the world. Businesses also have a vested interest in reminding people about it.

> **Function:**
> expressing future plans, hopes and wishes.
>
> **Grammar:**
> ▷ simple future and present continuous tenses, adverbs, modal verbs.
>
> ▷ conditionals – if ... then ...

We use the following expressions to talk about future plans.

The following phrases express a high degree of certainty:

I will	Tense choice
I'm going to	Tense choice
I have decided to	Tense choice + verb
I'm looking forward to	Tense choice + verb
I'm likely to	Adverb
I'll probably/possibly	Adverb

The following phrases express less certainty:

Perhaps/maybe I will	Adverb + verb tense
I am planning to	Tense choice + verb
I am hoping to	Tense choice + verb
I might	Modal verb
I could	Modal verb
I would (I'd) like to	Modal verb
If I pass my ... (then) I hope to	Conditional
If I had my way, (then) I would	Conditional

SPEAKING

TO WISH / TO HOPE

We use the phrases **to wish** and **to hope** to express future plans, dreams and desires. See the examples below and practise some of your own sentences.

to wish + past tense or infinitive finitive	to hope + simple present or infinitive
I wish I could fly.	I hope you have a happy birthday.
I wish he had warned me.	I hope he arrives safely.
I wish I were rich.	I hope you don't have any problems.
I wish to see the manager. May I see ... (here wish is polite for want).	In China I hope to see the Yangtse River.
	I hope to pass all my subjects.
I wish you a Merry Christmas. May I wish you a happy birthday.	I hope to get Band 7.0 in IELTS.

→ ## ACTIVITY 17

Fill in the blanks in the following sentences using the following words. You may use any word more than once.

hope	hoped	hopes	wish	wished	wishes

1 I _____ I could go home.

2 If I were rich I would fulfil all my _____ and dreams.

3 I _____ one day to be able to travel overseas.

4 Congratulations on getting married. I _____ you both all the happiness in the world!

5 The new *King Kong* was as good as I had _____ .

6 I need 6.5 in IELTS. I _____ I get it!

7 A friend of mine _____ to get a scholarship to an American university.

8 We _____ you a merry Christmas and a happy new year.

9 When I am in Spain I _____ to get to Bilbao to see the new Gehry building – the Guggenheim Museum.

10 I _____ I could design buildings like that!

Part One

Question:

What do you hope to do when you finish your studies?

SAMPLE
ANSWER

> **When I have finished** my studies I'm **going to** return home and look for work. I'm not sure what I'll do but I'm **hoping** to get a job as an assistant manager in a hotel. I'm **planning** to go to the capital city where there are more hotels and I'm more **likely** to find a job. I **wish** I had a bit more money, because then I would have a short holiday. I'm also **looking forward** to seeing my family again as I haven't been home for more than two years. I hope they don't think I've changed too much! **Maybe** they won't recognise me!

→ **ACTIVITY 18**

Complete the following by filling in the missing word/words. You may use some words more than once. There might be more than one right answer.

goal	to return	position	option	
would be	will	wish	alternatively	
when	job	otherwise	might	could

1 _____ my university course is over, I plan **2** _____ home and look for work. At the moment I'm not entirely sure what I **3** _____ do; I **4** _____ apply for a **5** _____ in an import-export business, ideally working in some way that I can use my English language skills. **6** _____ I **7** _____ take up a job in my father's company – he has a business manufacturing electrical components. One **8** _____ would be to start in a junior **9** _____ and learn about the business by working my way up through the different departments in the company.

10 _____ , I could begin work as a sales person in order to gain experience in marketing because my ultimate **11** _____ is to set up an export division for my father's firm and sell the company's products overseas, in Europe and South America. I **12** _____ I had an MBA, because then it **13** _____ a bit

SPEAKING

SPEAKING

SPECULATING means guessing about the future without knowing all the details or having access to all the relevant information, whereas **predicting** means using some information, some data or past experience to enable you to make a calculated guess. To **spec**ulate is to foresee (**spec**tator, **spec**tacles, in**spec**t etc) – to look into a crystal ball and attempt to see something.

To **PREDICT** means to "say before" (**pre + dict**), to work out what is going to happen based on past experience, or information supplied. Weather reporters can predict weather patterns, because they have access to relevant information. Those who read tarot cards and tell fortunes are merely speculating.

A speculator is someone who gambles on the possibility of property prices or shares increasing in value. We have a better chance of predicting earthquakes and volcanic eruptions these days because of advances in science.

Question:

How do you think people will communicate in 25 years' time?

SAMPLE ANSWER

> " It's very hard to imagine so far ahead. I **guess** that the internet **will be** even more popular. I **suppose** that mobile telephones will be more powerful and **will be able** to connect to the internet from anywhere. This **will probably** make calls easier, cheaper and faster. The quality **will hopefully be** better. Video links **should** also be more available. "

CALL TASK
www.australianetwork.com/studyenglish
Study English Series 1, Episode 16

SPEAKING

SPEAKING

Question:

Where do you think people might go for holidays in the future?

SAMPLE ANSWER

> Well, some very rich people are already flying into space, so space travel **might become** a possibility for more and more people. **If I had** enough money **I would** certainly **consider** a trip to the moon! I **wish** I had a few million dollars! The average person however **will still** want to see more of our planet and experience different cultures and landscapes, for example, New Zealand, where *'The Lord of the Rings'* was filmed. Personally speaking, I really want to travel around South America. I have always dreamt of travelling down the Amazon River, climbing up to Machu Picchu and gazing at the Iguazu Falls. I **hope** to get there one day. It **should be possible** as air fares are becoming cheaper all the time.

Question:

How do you think you will go in the test?

SAMPLE ANSWER

> Well, I've been studying very hard, and doing quite well in all the assignments. I'm a little worried about calculus. We **might** be given some difficult questions in the examination, and calculus is always tricky. However, based on all this I'm fairly confident. I **predict** I **will** at least pass, and **maybe** get a high grade, **just** as I **predicted** my team would win the last championship!

→ **ACTIVITY 19**

Complete the following statements using the words and phrases in the box.

guess	it's likely	I imagine	predict
	I would guess that	in the next generation	

1 _____ that with the doubling in the price of oil and petrol recently, more and more people will have to turn to public transport in the very near future.

2 I _____ that with the rise in temperatures, evaporation will also increase and thus rainfall will be affected.

3 In the next decade or so, _____ there will be considerable changes in workplaces and factories as new industrial relations regulations are put in place.

4 As the standard of living improves in China, so the number of nuclear families might become more common _____.

5 Well, I _____ as people work harder they will expect more leisure time and thus resorts and holiday destinations will proliferate.

6 With the spread of the flu virus _____ that sooner or later I will probably get sick.

Part Two

NOTE

Remember:

Fluency is speaking without too many pauses or hesitations, at a normal conversational speed.

Coherence means linking ideas and language together effectively through your answer. The examiner will listen for cohesive devices such as conjunctions, pronouns and connectors and a logical sequence of sentences and ideas.

PART TWO

In Part Two of the Speaking Test you are given a verbal prompt on a card and asked to talk for between one and two minutes. This is called the Individual Long Turn. You have one minute to prepare and you will be given paper and a pencil to write some notes.

At the end of your Long Turn the examiner might ask one or two follow-up questions – if there is enough time – to complete this section.

Part 2 and Part 3 of the IELTS Speaking Test focus on the criteria of Fluency and Coherence. This is because in these parts of the test your answers will be longer. In Part 1 of the test, short answers are expected. In a longer answer you have to think about how to organise your response. If you have problems with fluency and coherence, these will become apparent in a longer utterance.

This is an example of the sort of verbal prompt you might be given.

EXAMPLE

PRACTICE VERBAL PROMPT 1

Describe a subject you studied at school or university which you really enjoyed.

You should say:

▷ where you studied this subject

▷ how this subject was taught

▷ what was particularly interesting about this subject and explain how the ideas or theories you learnt have influenced you.

BRAINSTORM

Brainstorm the topic of education. Create headings relating to the topic, see examples below, and list relevant words for each heading.

EDUCATION

SUBJECTS: mathematics, science, biology, IT, business, English, history, religious studies, geography, economics, design, politics and society.

WHERE: primary, secondary, high school, college, university – undergraduate or post-graduate studies.

TEACHING METHOD: teacher, textbooks, exercises, presentations, lectures, tutorials, laboratories, group projects, individual projects, practical work, using videos, internet, online study.

ADJECTIVES: interesting, stimulating, inspiring, useful, practical, intellectual, intensive, challenging.

VALUES: It taught me to think, to empathise and increased my knowledge. It taught me the value of honesty, logic, made me appreciate my culture, other cultures and the value of working in a team. I learnt how to manage time and deal with money and people. I also learnt how to be creative, how to plan and manage a project.

TIP!

If you cannot remember a word or are hesitating, some of these words (fillers) might help you:

▷ actually

▷ anyway

▷ well, as I was saying

▷ in fact

▷ so

CALL TASK
www.australianetwork.com/studyenglish
Study English Series 1, Episode 15

Part Two

PRACTICE TASK 2

Look at the following prompt cards. Practise speaking for two minutes. Remember to time yourself.

PRACTICE VERBAL PROMPT 2

Describe something which you enjoy doing.

You should say:
▷ what it is
▷ why you enjoy doing it
▷ what equipment you need

and explain why you would suggest this activity to others.

TIP!

Look carefully at the prompts on your card. Make sure you talk about these and don't change the topic!

BRAINSTORM

Useful vocabulary: playing or watching sport, cooking, using a computer, online chatting, board games, reading, clubbing, shopping, karaoke

(This useful vocabulary will **not** be given to you in the exam!)

Check that you have:

▷ talked for between one and two minutes
▷ talked about each point in the question
▷ given examples.

TIP!

It's a good idea to record yourself when you practise speaking so you can check for grammar mistakes, pronunciation and fluency later, when you review what you have said.

TIP!

Do not try to memorise a speech on each topic!

If you memorise a prepared speech you will not score well in this section!

SAMPLE ANSWER

RESPONSE

Something which I really enjoy doing is listening to music – actually classical music and especially opera. I started late, even though I learnt to play the piano from the age of ten. My mother passed on her love of and interest in music, whether it was Broadway musicals like *'My Fair Lady'*, Handel's *'Messiah'*, or Puccini's *'La Boheme'*.

What it is

I suppose I enjoy listening to classical music because it is rousing – it lifts the spirits. It is also challenging as I must concentrate for a long time because classical music pieces are long. For example, piano concertos are approximately 30 minutes, while Wagner operas can be six hours long, requiring a meal break! However, it is worth it. There are some amazing climaxes in the classics. Einstein liked Bach and classical music too. He had fun working out the mathematics of Bach's Preludes and Fugues. My interests are a little more ordinary – pure enjoyment.

Why you enjoy doing it

The only equipment one needs is either a good stereo system to capture the quality of the recording, or otherwise something portable with earphones, such as an MP3 player. Of course you will also need a CD collection. I think I must own thousands of CDs.

What equipment you need

I think most people enjoy some classics already – Beethoven's *'Ode to Joy'* or whatever. I would recommend this activity to everyone because it is something we can do in the comfort of our own homes, in all weather, and it is calming and refreshing. It is good, clean fun for all.

Why you would suggest this activity to others

SPEAKING

115

Part Two

PRACTICE VERBAL PROMPT 3

Describe a person you have met who had a positive influence on your life.

You should say:
▷ where you met this person
▷ when the meeting took place
▷ how it was that you met this person

and explain what it was about this person that has had such an influence on you.

Grammar:
past tenses, time phrases, range of sentence types prepositions of time and place.

Vocabulary:
influence, behaviour, outlook, attitudes, inspire, motivate, educate, values, enthusiasm at school, at university, through my parents, through a friend, at work, by chance, he/she influenced my thinking, my behaviour, my outlook, my attitudes, my beliefs.

Part Two

Sometimes a response to the points in the prompt will not follow the exact order as outlined on the card. Look at this sample answer.

| **1 Introducing the person** | The person I would like to describe is one of the teachers I had at school. |

| **2 When the meeting took place** | So this is going back a few years now – maybe 10 or 15 years. I was much younger then! My family moved house and I had to go to a new school. Luckily it was better than the one I had been going to. It was in fact a very good school, and the students were on the whole very clever and gifted. |

| **3 Where you met this person** | The English teacher we had at that school was truly inspirational. My younger brothers also had him as a teacher, but it seemed the students in my year were most influenced by him. It was a mutually inspiring interaction. Actually I should not have had him as my teacher because I was at first placed in a lower level, but I managed to change class and join my classmate. |

| **4 How it was that you met this person** | This teacher gave us a love of English literature, that also might have been helped by the syllabus – great Shakespeare plays like *'Hamlet'*, *'Antony and Cleopatra'* and *'Romeo and Juliet'*; great poets such as Keats and Yeats; and great novelists such as Dickens, Bronte and Austen. |

| **5 What it was about this person that has had such an influence on you?** | Not only was he enthusiastic about the literature but he was able to communicate and explain his feelings or judgements to the class. He treated us like adults – respecting our feelings and responses, but leading and guiding us at the same time – probing, challenging, clarifying. The personal touch and the respect he showed made the difference I think – helping to define a great teacher as one who engages with and inspires his students. He actually helped me establish a moral awareness, and my critical sensibilities, and then learn how to articulate these, verbally and in writing. |

→ **ACTIVITY 20**

Complete the following response by choosing suitable words from the box.

enthusiastic	amazing	excited	interesting
envious	surprised	enjoying	huge

What really **1** _____ me when I started my university studies last week was the **2** _____ diversity of people in my class. There were students from many parts of the world! I find this such a **3** _____ benefit because working closely with people from diverse backgrounds really helps me to learn about other cultures. I was also **4** _____ to find that there were some students in my class from my own country, although I'm determined not to restrict my socialising to this group. I'm really **5** _____ of people who speak other languages fluently, and I'm so **6** _____ about improving my own ability to speak to people in another language. In my opinion, this is a really important skill in the international world of work and study today. I've only been in this class for one week but already I'm really **7** _____ it and can't wait to see where it leads me! The course itself also looks **8** _____ too!

SPEAKING

→ ACTIVITY 21

Choose from the following phrases to complete the sentences below.

biggest	as much	more ... than
more ... than	least	most
not so many ... as	as many ... as	the same ... as
greater ... than		

1 It is obvious that the Mexicans spend _____ money on developing and maintaining their subway system _____ Los Angeles, for example.

2 The _____ popular mode of transport, however, is the motor car.

3 Mexico city has nearly _____ population _____ Sao Paulo, Brazil.

4 There are almost _____ people living in greater Los Angeles _____ in Mexico city.

5 I spent a _____ amount of time in the Templo Mayor museum _____ outside, inspecting the temple site.

6 The _____ surprise of my visit was the visit to Teotihuacan, where I saw the great Pyramids of the Sun and Moon.

7 There are apparently _____ Aztec ruins in Mexico _____ there are in Guatemala.

8 It seems _____ people in Latin America play football _____ watch it, and then they spend nearly _____ time talking about it afterwards.

9 The _____ well-known or appreciated fact about Los Angeles is its excellent bus system.

SPEAKING

PREPOSITIONS OF TIME

 ACTIVITY 22

Complete the following recount by choosing the correct prepositions of time.

at	in	ago

I have been to Russia a couple of times. The first time was **1** _____ 1979, **2** _____ winter, **3** _____ January, just **4** _____ the time of the orthodox Christmas. The last time was a few years **5** _____ , **6** _____ the beginning of this century, or the new millennium, this time **7** _____ summer – actually **8** _____ the end of May, beginning of June. The first time I went I flew in, but on this occasion I travelled by train. I arrived **9** _____ the morning, just as people in Moscow were going to work. I arrived **10** _____ my hotel **11** _____ about 9:00. I telephoned a few friends and that night we met for dinner **12** _____ 8 o'clock **13** _____ the evening. It's not unusual for me to stay up late **14** _____ night, but that night I was really tired, so I turned in early.

PRACTICE PROMPT CARDS

PRACTICE VERBAL PROMPT 4

Describe a traditional celebration which you know well.

You should say:
▷ where the ceremony is held
▷ what the purpose of the ceremony is
▷ what you feel about it

and explain why this ceremony is important to you.

Grammar:
present and perfect tenses, time phrases, range of sentence types, prepositions of time and place.

Vocabulary:
engagements, weddings, marriages, birthdays, funerals, New Year's Eve, festivals, religious ceremonies in temples, mosques or shrines, blessings and offerings, services.

PRACTICE VERBAL PROMPT 5

Describe a place you have enjoyed visiting.

You should say:
▷ where this place is located
▷ how you came to go there
▷ why you enjoyed it

and explain why you would recommend this place to others.

Grammar:
past tenses, time phrases, range of sentence types, prepositions of time and place.

Vocabulary:
a foreign country, a local town, place of natural beauty, a national park, a garden, the coast, a beach, markets, shopping malls, a restaurant or bar, a theme park, zoo, a national landmark, a historic site.

PRACTICE VERBAL PROMPT 6

Describe your favourite building.

You should say:
▷ where this building is
▷ what it looks like
▷ what it is used for

and say why this building attracts you.

Grammar:
present tense for describing things, range of sentence types
It is made of ...
It looks like ...
It has a rectangular/square/oval shape
It has ...
It is ...
It was designed and built by ...

Vocabulary:
office block, highrise, apartment block, tower, opera house, concert hall, museum, theatre, cinema, palace, monument, temple, cathedral, mosque, shrine, traditional house.

PRACTICE VERBAL PROMPT 7

Describe something which you find annoying.

You should say:
▷ what it is
▷ why it irritates you
▷ how other people feel about this

and make suggestions to deal with this problem.

PRACTICE VERBAL PROMPT 8

Describe an example of serious pollution.

You should say:
▷ where it is
▷ what made you notice it
▷ what makes you think it is serious

and explain what you think could be done to prevent it.

PRACTICE VERBAL PROMPT 9

Describe a feature of the education system in your country.

You should say:
▷ what it is
▷ why you find it interesting
▷ what makes it important and special

and say how this feature might be used in other countries.

Practice Prompt Cards

PRACTICE VERBAL PROMPT 10

Describe someone you admire.

You should say:
▷ who this person is
▷ why you admire them
▷ how they impact you

and say which attributes inspire you in your own life.

PRACTICE VERBAL PROMPT 11

Describe your favourite restaurant.

You should say:
▷ where this restaurant is
▷ why you like it
▷ what you usually order

and say why you would recommend this restaurant

PRACTICE VERBAL PROMPT 12

Describe a film you have seen recently and enjoyed.

You should say:
▷ the name of the film and who was in it
▷ what the film was about
▷ why you enjoyed it

and say why you would recommend this film to others.

PART THREE

In Part Three the examiner and the candidate discuss more abstract ideas which are linked by theme or topic to the verbal prompt used in Part Two. (An abstract idea is more theoretical than real). This part of the test lasts between four and five minutes.

PREPARING FOR PART THREE

You will do better in Part Three if you are able to discuss ideas in depth. These activities will help you to improve your fluency and develop your ideas.

In Part Three the examiner and the candidate are involved in a discussion. When we discuss, we:

▷ talk about what is and what might be (speculation and prediction)

▷ explain how we feel about something (comment)

▷ make suggestions and give opinions

▷ try to persuade people to see things differently.

In a discussion we usually cannot be completely certain about what we say. In formal discussions we have to learn to be objective, tentative and polite.

So, to prepare for Part 3 of the IELTS Speaking Test, there are several skills requiring development, and language functions to practise.

SKILLS

Organising Longer Responses

LANGUAGE FUNCTIONS

1. Speculation and prediction
2. Expressing degrees of certainty
3. Giving opinions
4. Expressing conditions
5. Making suggestions

ORGANISING LONGER RESPONSES

Remember in the IELTS Speaking Test do not just answer with a short simple response.

Extend your answer using examples, giving reasons, adding information and explaining.

Give: **E**xtra **E**vidence

          Explanations

          Examples

CALL TASK
www.australianetwork.com/studyenglish
Study English Series 2, Episode 11

SPEAKING

**SAMPLE
ANSWERS**

Reason

" I imagine that over the next decade working conditions will change quite dramatically. The chief reason for this is the new Industrial Relations legislation that the current government is putting before parliament. "

Evidence

" There will be a few changes in the way we spend our leisure time in the near future. For example, families will be smaller and therefore parents will be able to afford traveling further, such as to other countries. This will be evident in more holiday packages being constructed by travel companies, and discounts offered for small families. "

Explanation or clarification

" In developing countries the extended family is still very much the norm. By this I mean that most families have several children, and grandparents or aunts and uncles either living together or close by. It is usually only in developed countries where we find nuclear families – **that is**, a mother, father and child/children, living independently. "

" With the increase in the price of petrol people will think carefully about driving long distances to work or for a holiday. In addition, car companies will be producing smaller, cleaner and more fuel efficient engines. **I feel** that this will, in the end, be much better for the environment and the planet. "

Comment

CALL TASK
www.australianetwork.com/studyenglish
Study English Series 2, Episode 3

PREPARE FOR IELTS: Skills and Strategies   INSEARCH ENGLISH

SPEAKING

SPEAKING

1 SPECULATION AND PREDICTION

When we talk about what might be, we do not know what the answer will be. This is called speculation and prediction. Refer back to page 109.

2 EXPRESSING DEGREES OF CERTAINTY

We can use the following phrases to express degrees of certainty.

 ACTIVITY 23

Number these phrases 1-11 in order of strength, with 1 being the strongest.

Expressing degrees of certainty	
Perhaps	There could be ...
Maybe	I expect that ...
Probably	I'm quite sure that ...
Possibly	I believe that ...
Undoubtedly	I'm fairly sure that ...
I guess that ...	

TIP!

If you use the correct grammar to talk about future possibilities, you are likely to improve your speaking results.

 **EXAMPLE**

Look at the example.

> I'm **not sure** what I'll be doing in 2010 but I'm **fairly sure** I'll be married and **possibly** have one or two children. I **expect** that I'll be living in my home town and **perhaps** we **will** have our own business.

 BRAINSTORM

Think about the following. How would you talk about these topics using speculative language?

▷ What will you be doing in ten years' time?

▷ Do you think there will be an oil crisis in the future?

▷ Will English continue to be a major international language?

▷ Do you think the tourism industry in your country will increase or decrease?

SPEAKING

3 GIVING OPINIONS

LANGUAGE BOX

PHRASES

▷ In my opinion, ...

▷ In my view, ...

▷ To my mind, ...

VERBS

▷ I believe ...

▷ I think ...

▷ I feel ...

MODAL VERBS

▷ In my opinion, there should be ...

▷ I believe the government should ...

▷ I strongly feel that teachers must ...

Question:

Why do you think the crime rate is increasing in developing countries?

SAMPLE ANSWER

"   **It seems to me that** inflation and lack of job opportunities are the main factors that have produced an increase in the crime rate in many developing countries. I believe inflation is a big problem because many people who work don't make enough money to live and, what's more important, to educate their children. Also **I feel** the lack of job opportunities is another main cause of increasing crime. Unemployed people have no way to get food or even a place to live because many governments do not provide any social services to the poor. I **really believe** that poverty is one of the main reasons why people turn to crime. **In my opinion**, governments of developing countries must stabilise their currencies and build factories to employ people so that the crime rates drop. "

SPEAKING

→ **ACTIVITY 24**

Complete the following by choosing the correct word from the box.

wouldn't	I believe	couldn't	might
should	in my opinion	may	could

1 The question whether the age of drivers _____ be lowered has been hotly debated over the years.

2 Captial punishment, _____ , does not act as a deterrent for drug smugglers.

3 The volunteers have demonstrated on numerous occasions that they _____ be effective fire fighters.

4 Although I have studied the language for many years, I _____ understand a word he said because of his heavy accent.

5 Nutritionists believe that eating more fish _____ assist in the management of asthma.

6 _____ , the government needs to regulate the price of petrol.

7 I was thinking we _____ do the bushwalk along the coast with our overseas visitors.

8 Deregulating the industry _____ be a politically expedient solution because of the backlash from the factory workers.

SPEAKING

129

SPEAKING

4 EXPRESSING CONDITIONS

By using "if" clauses (conditionals) in English we are able to introduce the condition which an action depends upon. For example: If I run late, will you take notes for me?

EXAMPLE

Worker:	We demand a 17% salary increase.
Manager:	I will agree to that if you increase productivity by as much.
Worker:	Would you agree to 10% now and 7% next financial year?
Manager:	Yes, I would agree to that only if you agreed to my terms.

What is the difference between these two Conditionals?

1	I will ... if you agree to	will + simple present
2	I would agree to ... if you did	would + past tense

The first conditional is more certain – there will definitely be an outcome if some particular event takes place.

The second conditional is more tentative, more polite, more conditional, less certain.

EXAMPLE

> If it rains tomorrow, I will stay home.

The decision is clear. It rains, then I stay home. Simple.

EXAMPLE

> I would if I could, but I can't, so I won't!

> On what condition would you be prepared to walk a mile to the beach?

> I would walk a mile to the beach:
>
> if it was a hot day.
> if I knew I could get a bus back.
> if it was the only way I could see my friends, etc.

CALL TASK
www.australianetwork.com/studyenglish
Study English Series 1, Episode 14

SPEAKING

PRACTICE TASK 3

To gain confidence in using the second conditional, prepare a response to the following questions:

On what condition would you:

▷ shave your head?

▷ let somebody borrow your passport?

▷ use an internet dating service?

▷ get a tattoo?

PRACTICE TASK 4

Talk for one or two minutes on each of the following questions.

If you were ...

▷ the Secretary-General of the United Nations

▷ the Minister for Health in your country

▷ an expert on computer viruses

▷ Minister for Education in your home country

▷ the Chief of Police in your capital city

▷ your favourite pop star

What would be the first three things you would do?

You might begin 'If I were the Secretary-General of the United Nations, I would ...'

SPEAKING

5 MAKING SUGGESTIONS

GRAMMAR BOX

Verbs	I suggest/propose
Question	Why don't you ...? Have you tried/thought about ...?
Modal verbs	May I suggest You might try It might be possible to You should You could always Some people have done ... You could try that.
Adverbs	Maybe/perhaps we could

PRACTICE TASK 5

Practise for your Speaking Test by preparing responses to the following scenarios:

▷ Your friend wants to go home before the end of his course of study. Suggest reasons why this is or is not a good idea.

▷ Your friend can't decide where to go for dinner. Suggest a place where you like to eat.

▷ Your friend wants to marry somebody who is a lot older/younger. Suggest reasons why this is or is not a good idea.

PRACTICE TASK 6

Choose one of these topics and speak for up to two minutes. Be ready to justify your position.

▷ If you could choose any city in the world, which city would you live in, and why?

▷ How do you think living in 100 years' time will be different to now?

▷ In the field of medical research, what do we need to spend the most money on in the next ten years?

▷ What criticisms would you make of the education system in which you were educated?

▷ Do you think children's emotional and intellectual development will be adversely affected by computer games?

▷ Should environmental laws be applied equally to developed and developing economies?

END OF THE INTERVIEW

▷ How do you think the examiner will signal that the interview is over?

▷ What words might the examiner use?

▷ What body language or gestures might the examiner use?

▷ At the end of the interview, you say goodbye to the examiner and leave. The examiner cannot tell you what your score is, so please do not ask.

IELTS Results are usually available within two weeks. The Test Report Form (TRF) will give you a result for each of the four tests, and an overall band score.

/θæŋkt/

CLARITY

COHERENCE

/laft/

FLUENCY

INTONATION

STRESS

FLUENCY

CLARITY

SOUNDS

/danst/

COMMUNICATION

FLUENCY

RHYTHM

CLARITY

SPEAKING

SPEAKING

PRACTICE TASK 7
Listen to each of the sample speaking interviews on CD 3
in **Prepare for IELTS: Academic Practice Tests**. Using the
Speaking Skills Report Work Sheet, assess each of the
sample speaking interviews.

1 PRODUCTION SKILLS

PRONUNCIATION	Assessment	Comments
Rhythm Number and length of pauses	1 2 3	
Stress	1 2 3	
Intonation	1 2 3	
Sounds	1 2 3	

2 COMMUNICATION SKILLS

SPEAKING	Assessment	Comments
Fluency	1 2 3	
Clarity	1 2 3	
Coherence	1 2 3	
Confidence	1 2 3	
Cultural Appropriacy	1 2 3	

3 LANGUAGE SKILLS

LANGUAGE	Assessment	Comments
Grammatical Accuracy	1 2 3	
Grammatical Range	1 2 3	
Vocabulary Range	1 2 3	

▷ **1** = needs more attention **2** = satisfactory **3** = good

SPEAKING

Speech Analysis Form

NAME: _____

DATE OF BIRTH: _____ NATIONALITY: _____

EDUCATION: _____ (years) LEVEL (eg secondary, tertiary): _____

SPEECH ANALYSIS

VOWELS & DIPHTHONGS

SHORT VOWELS	æ	ʌ	ɜ	ə	ɪ	ɒ	ʊ
LONG VOWELS		a		ɜ	i	ɔ	u

DIPHTHONGS			
	ɛə	aɪ	aʊ
	ɪə	ɪə	oʊ
	ʊə	ɔɪ	

SEMI-VOWELS or GLIDES	w
	r
	j

CONSONANTS

UNVOICED	p	f	θ	t	s	ʃ	tʃ	k
VOICED	b	v	ð	d	z	ʒ	dʒ	g
LATERAL					l			h
NASALS	m			n				ŋ

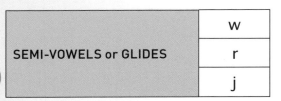

SPEAKING

Speech Analysis Form

SUGGESTIONS

SOUNDS
List problem sounds and identify position (initial or final).

_____

_____

_____

_____

_____

_____

STRESS
Syllable and sentence stress.

_____

_____

_____

_____

_____

_____

INTONATION
Falling and rising intonation.

_____

_____

_____

_____

_____

_____

FLUENCY
Amount of pausing, linking, smooth speech, etc.

_____

_____

_____

_____

_____

SPEAKING

Vocabulary Work Sheet 1

TOPIC: _____

SUBTOPIC	VOCABULARY

QUESTIONS YOU COULD BE ASKED	FUNCTION
1	
2	
3	
4	
5	
6	
7	
8	
9	
10	

▷ Now, practise answering each of these questions. Don't forget to time your responses!

SPEAKING

TOPIC: _____

WORD FORM	VOCABULARY
ADJECTIVES	
NOUNS	
VERBS	
ADVERBS	

QUESTIONS YOU COULD BE ASKED	FUNCTION
1	
2	
3	
4	
5	
6	
7	
8	
9	
10	

▷ Now, practise answering each of these questions. Don't forget to time your responses!

PHOTOCOPYING PERMITTED
You may **photocopy** this page.

SPEAKING

Topics

Talk about your family.	Talk about pets.
What do you enjoy most in life?	What are you most afraid of?
Talk about your favourite television program.	Describe your favourite clothes.
Talk about your best friend.	What is your favourite food?
Talk about what you most like to eat for lunch.	Talk about your last birthday.
Talk about a funny experience.	Talk about someone you love.
Talk about a strange experience.	Talk about someone you dislike.
Talk about a sport.	Talk about your feelings on shopping.
Talk about what you do every day.	Talk about a favourite film.
Tell the class how to cook a simple dish.	Talk about what you usually do on the weekend.
Talk about your first day in Australia.	What are some of the problems you have learning English?
Talk about what you remember most clearly about studying English last week.	Talk about your favourite teacher.
Talk about a happy experience.	Talk about your first day at school.
Talk about your feelings on technology.	Talk about your favourite subject at school or university.
Talk about someone you admire.	Talk about a frightening experience.
What is your first memory?	Talk about what you most like to eat for breakfast.
Talk about a goal you have.	Talk about an important leader in your country.

PREPARE FOR IELTS: Skills and Strategies INSEARCH ENGLISH

SPEAKING

140

SPEAKING

Topics

Talk about a goal you have.	Talk about an important leader in your country.
Talk about a famous singer or movie star.	Talk about your idea of a good holiday.
Talk about your mobile phone.	Talk about a good place to visit in your country.
Talk about the number of students from your country studying overseas.	Talk about studying at home and studying overseas.
Talk about your favourite fast food in your country.	Talk about an important custom in your country.
Talk about what your country is famous for.	Talk about how modern technology has affected your country.
Talk about a famous person.	Talk about your thoughts on education.
Talk about a happy holiday.	What do you believe is the best way to learn English?
Talk about what you do every day.	Talk about your habits.
Talk about how your family feel about your future study.	Talk about the main industries in your country.
Talk about your future career.	Talk about computer games.

SPEAKING

Compare two well-known buildings in the city you are in now.	Compare being a student at high school and being a student now as an adult.
Compare home-cooked meals and takeaway food.	Compare two kinds of popular drinks.
Compare the roles of men and women in your country.	Compare living at home with living away from home.
Compare watching TV and going to the movies.	Compare two kinds of music.
Compare growing up in the 21st century to the time your grandparents grew up.	Compare two seaons in your country.
Compare your town/city now to when you were growing up.	Compare your country with a neighbouring country.
Compare learning as a child and learning as an adult.	Compare family life in your country and another country.
Compare your home town with another town.	Compare the advantages of public transport versus cars, or vice versa.
Compare tea and coffee.	Compare a traditional house in your country with modern accommodation.
Compare two sports.	Compare different ways of exercising.

SPEAKING

Topics

DISCUSS

Discuss how what we eat has changed over the last twenty years.	Discuss how holidays have changed in your country.
Discuss tourism in your country, now and in the future.	Discuss what your country produces.

DESCRIBE

Describe an important festival in your country.	Describe the education system in your country.
Describe your favourite place.	Describe your favourite clothes.
Describe a traditional dish from your country.	Describe where you live now.
Describe your home town/city.	Describe your favourite place in the city you live in now.
Describe your favourite building.	Describe your favourite season.

MORE TOPICS

The three things I hope to achieve in my life.	The things people will value most in the year 2020.
The most important medical discovery of all time.	My reasons for choosing my particular course of study.
Success in the job market is impossible without a university degree. Ambition alone will not allow you to achieve what you want. Discuss.	The changes you would most like to see in the circumstances of foreign students.
In sport as in business, winning is the only result that matters.	The importance of family life as the basic unit of society.
The importance of development for countries in your region.	The contribution sporting contests make to relationships between countries.
The benefits of modern technology to developing countries and developed countries.	What are the responsibilities of youth in today's society?

TRANSCRIPTS & ANSWERS

LISTENING 1

Narrator: Activity 1: 'About the Listening Test'. Listen to this conversation about the IELTS listening test.

Candidate: Excuse me. You're teaching people how to sit for the IELTS listening test, is that right?

Teacher: Yeah, that's right.

Candidate: Can I ask you some questions about the test? I have to take it in two months time.

Teacher: Sure. I'd be glad to help.

Candidate: First, I'd like to ask you about the length of the test.

Teacher: Okay. The test is usually about 30 minutes long, that's fairly standard, and it contains around 40 questions.

Candidate: Forty questions. Is that all one continuous conversation?

Teacher: No, no, it's divided into four sections.

Candidate: Are all the sections on the same topic?

Teacher: Each section is on a different topic and has different voices, and what you hear in each section could be in several parts of, I suppose, about a minute or two, or it might be all the one thing, say a conversation that goes for four or five minutes.

Candidate: Okay, and what about time in between each section?

Teacher: Well, between each section first of all you'll have the instructions, which are all given on tape, and then usually you'll be given, well always you'll be given, thirty seconds or so to read over the questions, then you'll hear the tape and answer the questions as you hear it. You only get it once so you have to listen very carefully. That's very important.

Candidate: Oh, only once.

Teacher: Yeah, only once, and then at the end of each section they'll give you 30 seconds to check over your answers, and again at the end of the entire test they'll give you some time to look back over the answers for the test.

Candidate: Right. What about the content of the test? What am I going to hear?

Teacher: Well, again it varies but it tends to be taken from two general areas. In the earlier sections, the first two, it's usually from survival kind of situations, I mean the type of experiences students would have when they arrive in a foreign country, like getting ready to start your course.

Candidate: Or checking in at a hotel or a dorm?

Teacher: Yeah, that's right, things like that, asking directions, arranging to meet people, that kind of thing, and then in the later part of the test, which is generally more difficult, the passages are usually taken from some academic kind of situation so it could be somebody ... part of a lecture, for example ... or it could be somebody introducing library facilities, or explaining how to get a student card. That kind of thing.

Candidate: Okay, and what about the accents? Do they have British accents?

Teacher: No, there could be British accents on it or there could be Australian or American or, say, Canadian. You could have quite a range of accents, although they wouldn't be too strong but you have to be ready for that. And they'll be male and female voices on the tape. It could be, also, a monologue if someone's giving a lecture, for example.

Candidate: What's a monologue?

Teacher: A monologue means just one person will be talking.

Candidate: Right.

Teacher: But it could also be dialogue ... a couple of people discussing what they're going to do that evening or something like that. Usually the first section is a dialogue, you know, a conversation between two people, and then you'll usually hear another conversation in Section Three.

Candidate: Okay. Well, the last thing I'd like to ask is about the type of questions you get.

Teacher: Okay. Here they've really tried to make a variety of different types of questions to test people. So there might be some questions which have a graphic format. There could be pictures to choose from, there might be a chart where you have to fill in information, or a table. You'll probably have some multiple choice in there somewhere. You'll almost certainly at some point have to write in some answers which could be single words, or a cloze test for example, where you have to fill in the gaps of a test, or it might be filling in a few words. You might have to fill in a form, for example putting down addresses or times or dates, or information like that. Or you might have to write down short answers to questions, but you never have to write more than three words.

Candidate: Do you always write down exactly what you hear on the tape?

Teacher: Not necessarily. A lot of the pieces are organised so that you can't copy down exactly what you hear word for word. They're trying to check the candidates' understanding of meaning, so you have to listen carefully for the meaning, but when you're filling in a cloze test, a gap-fill for example, you might have to use other words which still convey the meaning of what you heard.

Candidate: Where do you write the answers? Can I write on the exam paper?

Teacher: Yes, you can. You have to write your answers on the paper and then at the end of the test you have to transfer your answers to the answer sheet. You get time to do this and the instructions are always clear. But you've got to be careful when you're doing it so you don't get the questions mixed up.

Candidate: Right. Okay, well, thank you very much. I feel more confident now about the listening part of the test.

Teacher: I'm sure you'll do well. Good luck.

Candidate: Thank you very much.

LISTENING 2

Narrator: Activity 2: 'Passenger Survey'.

Market Researcher (MR): Excuse me, Madam, could I get you to answer some questions about Route 440?

Respondent (Resp): Will it take long? I have to get off soon.

MR: It should only take about five minutes.

Resp: Okay.

MR: Thanks. Hmm. Today's date is the 15th of May, isn't it?

Resp: Yes, that's right.

MR: Okay. Thanks. The first question is: how often do you travel on this bus route? Less than once a month, daily, twice a day, more than twice a day?

Resp: I use this route twice daily. Once on my way to work, and once on my way home.

MR: So are you going to work now?

Resp: No, I'm not. I'm going to the movies.

MR: Thanks. Now I have to ask you to rate the service on a scale of 1 to 4: 1 is very bad and 4 is very good. First of all, punctuality: is the bus on time? 1 is very bad …

Resp: It used to be good, but during the last few weeks it's been very unreliable. Say 1.

MR: What about the comfort of the bus?

Resp: Well, this one is okay, but some of the older buses on route 440 are very uncomfortable. I'd say 2.

MR: What about the cost?

Resp: I travel from the beginning of one section to the end of the other, so the cost is okay. I'd say 3.

MR: Is the bus clean?

Resp: Usually it's fairly clean in the morning, but it deteriorates during the day, and it's quite dirty on the way home. Can I give it two scores, one for the morning and one for the afternoon?

MR: Sorry. The computer can only read one score here.

Resp: I'll give it a 2.

MR: Last question: how do you rate the service from the staff?

Resp: Really good. Let them have a 4. The drivers are always polite, and the passengers can be very difficult.

MR: Thank you very much for helping.

LISTENING 4

Narrator: Activity 4: 'Word Endings'. You will hear 10 sets of three words. Circle the word you hear twice. For example, if you hear '18 80 18', you will circle '18'. Now we will begin:

1	15	50	15
2	bend	bent	bent
3	led	let	led
4	word	work	work
5	16	60	60
6	dish	ditch	ditch
7	bed	bet	bet
8	13	30	13
9	seal	seal	seam
10	slim	slim	slip

LISTENING 5

Narrator: Activity 5: 'Numbers'. You will hear ten numbers in these conversations. Write these numbers down as you hear them.

1

Speaker 1: Directory assistance, can I help you?

Speaker 2: Yes. I'd like the number for interstate directory assistance.

Speaker 1: Yes, it's 1175 (double one seven five).

2

Speaker: Please call me at home after 6. My number is 9555 6140 (9555 614 oh).

3

Speaker 1: What's the number for the snow report, please?

Speaker 2: It's 0055 12370 (double oh double five, one two three seven oh).

4

Speaker 1: Do you know the number for transport services?

Speaker 2: Yes, it's 131 500 (one three one five hundred).

5

Speaker 1: Could I have the number for the Accommodation Service?

Speaker 2: Yes, it's a 1 800 number, 1 800 666 9181 (one eight hundred, six six six, nine one eight one).

6

Speaker: His phone number at work is 672 3000 (six seven two three thousand).

7

Speaker: The number for the translating service is 13 13 50 (one three one three five zero).

8

Speaker 1: What was that fax number again?

Speaker 2: 973 7333 (nine seven three seven triple three).

9

Speaker 1: What's your fax number in Vienna?

Speaker 2: It's 43 for Austria, 1 201 316 809 (one two oh one three one six eight oh nine).

Speaker 1: Was that 43 1 201 316 809?

Speaker 2: That's right.

10.

Speaker 1: The emergency number for the crime hotline is 1 800 025 121 (one eight hundred, zero two five, one two one).

Speaker 2: Thanks.

LISTENING 6

Narrator: Activity 6: 'Dates'. You will hear ten dates. Write the dates you hear.

1

Speaker: Johan Sebastian Bach was born on the 21st of March 1685.

2

Speaker: Omar Sharif's birthday is April 10th.

3

Speaker: The enrolment date is February the 21st.

4

Speaker: He was born sometime in the 90s.

5

Speaker: Did you say the 30th of September?

6

Speaker: The morning of the 8th of November will be fine.

7

Speaker: How did people travel around in the 16th century?

8

Speaker: It was finished in November 1853.

9

Speaker: War broke out on December 1st, 1950.

10

Speaker: The public holiday is on the fourteenth of July.

LISTENING 7

Narrator: Activity 7: 'Fractions, Percentages, Money and Decimals'. You will hear ten numbers. Write every fraction, percentage, decimal number and amount of money you hear. You should indicate any currency you hear.

1

Speaker 1: The recipe calls for two-thirds of a cup of rice.

Speaker 2: That's a pity. We're fresh out.

2

Speaker 1: That's 12 and a half per cent, then.

Speaker 2: Correct.

3

Speaker 1: Do you have $50? I've lost my money.

Speaker 2: OK.

4

Speaker 1: A kilometre is five-eighths of a mile.

Speaker 2: Are you sure? I thought it was more than that.

5

Speaker 1: Did you know that 38.65% of samples were affected?

Speaker 2: Are you sure?

6

Speaker 1: That horse was sold for £750.

Speaker 2: That's not bad.

7

Speaker 1: The average American family has 2.2 children.

Speaker 2: Is it the same in Canada?

8

Speaker 1: On the map, only 0.3% (point three per cent) of the total area shows up as being in use.

Speaker 2: Is that all?

9

Speaker 1: The government paid $530 million for that.

Speaker 2: You mean the taxpayer paid!

10

Speaker 1: How did you get on?

Speaker 2: I scored 85.5%!

LISTENING 9

Narrator: Activity 9: 'Spelling Places and Names'. Write every name or place name that you hear.

1

Speaker: I'm going to Missouri. That's M-I-S-S-O-U-R-I.

2

Speaker: The capital is Canberra, C-A-N-B-E-double R-A.

3

Speaker: Please send this to Harry Luske, that's H-A-R-R-Y L-U-S-K-E.

4

Speaker: Write to me in Johannesburg. J-O-H-A-double N-E-S-B-U-R-G.

5

Speaker: In your atlas, look up Vancouver, V-A-N-C-O-U-V-E-R.

6

Speaker: Her name is Maria Strella. I'll spell the family name, S-T-R-E-L-L-A.

7

Speaker: Bill McLean spells his surname capital M-small-C-capital L-E-A-N.

8

Speaker: The restaurant is called Sammy's, that's S-A-M-M-Y apostrophe S.

9

Speaker: We live near Runnymede, that's R-U-double -N-Y-M-E-D-E.

10

Speaker: My teacher is Professor Kumar, K-U-M-A-R.

LISTENING 10

Narrator: Activity 10: 'Tasks which involve Graphs'. Listen and write A B C or D to indicate the chart or graph being discussed.

1

Lecturer: Please look at the graphs which show the types of waste we are dealing with in four different cities. Fortunately for us our city has the least toxic waste of them all.

2

Teacher: The bar graph I want you to look at shows the largest column in the middle, with the smallest amounts at either end.

3

Accountant: These figures show our sales for the year. As you can see, we did best in April and showed very little variation during the rest of the year.

LISTENING 12

Narrator: Activity 12: 'Listening for Specific Detail in Descriptions of People'. Listen to the taped descriptions of the people in the illustrations A–H. Match the descriptions to the pictures.

Narrator: Person Number 1.

Speaker: The first person is John Edwards. John is 40 years old and works in an office. He is not very tall and he is of medium-build. His hair is thinning but he is not bald. He is clean-shaven. He likes to wear a bow-tie with his suit and usually carries an umbrella or a cane.

Narrator: Person Number 2.

Speaker: The second person is Gwen Charles. She likes to wear casual clothes that she can be comfortable in, but she always looks tidy and rather conservative. She has short, dark, straight hair and a pleasant face.

Narrator: Person Number 3.

Speaker: The third person is Sally Valdes. Sally has been married for two years; she married very young. Before her marriage she was a photographer, but now she only works occasionally in her profession. She dresses very casually and has short, curly hair.

Narrator: Person Number 4.

Speaker: The fourth person is Matthew Lee. Matthew is 17 and still in high school. He doesn't enjoy school very much and looks forward to the time when his studies will be finished. He prefers to dress in very casual clothes like jeans and T-shirts.

Narrator: Person Number 5.

Speaker: The fifth person is William Poinkin. Mr Poinkin retired from his job when he reached the age of 65. He still dresses very conservatively, and enjoys wearing a suit. He is almost bald but is very proud of his moustache.

Narrator: Person Number 6.

Speaker: The sixth person is Teresa Blake. Mrs Blake has been a school teacher for the last thirty years. She dresses in very practical clothes because she says there is no sense in wearing fashionable clothes or good jewellery to work because they just get ruined. She has had to wear glasses for some years now.

Narrator: Person Number 7.

Speaker: The seventh person's name is Margaret Connors. Margaret is a university student. She is studying politics at the moment but hopes to change to law. She likes to wear loose, casual clothes and is very tall with long hair. She also likes to wear jewellery.

Narrator: Person Number 8.

Speaker: Andrew Janacek is the eighth person. Andrew is a bus-driver, aged 23. In his spare time he plays a lot of soccer. He plays several other sports as well because he tries to keep as fit as possible, but soccer is what he really loves. He wears his hair fairly long and has a short beard.

LISTENING 13

Narrator: Activity 13: 'Completing Forms'. Listen to the dialogue and fill out the application form while you listen.

Interviewer: I need to ask you some questions so I can fill out this form. Could I have your name, please? I need your family name first.

Applicant: My family name is Calvi. You spell that C-A-L-V-I. My first name is Mario, that's M-A-R-I-O.

Interviewer: Any other names?

Applicant: No.

Interviewer: What's your nationality?

Applicant: Italian.

Interviewer: So your first language is Italian?

Applicant: No, actually it's not! My first language is German.

Interviewer: Thanks. How long have you studied English?

Applicant: Quite a long time. About ten years.

Interviewer: How much education have you had? Have you finished high school?

Applicant: Of course. I've completed a graduate diploma in nursing.

Interviewer: That's good. When would you like to do the test?

Applicant: Is there a test available in August?

Interviewer: August 13, 19 and 30 are all test days. You have to nominate two.

Applicant: Then I'd like to do it on the 13th, and if that can't be done, make it the 30th.

LISTENING 14

Narrator: Activity 14: 'Moving to a New Campus'. The speaker is explaining the process of a move to a new campus. As you listen, answer questions 1–7 by marking T for true and F for false.

Manager: Good morning, ladies and gentlemen. I've called this meeting to discuss our new campus which is opening fully next year. We plan to move our students to the new facilities in groups, so please listen carefully. The Agricultural Science students won't move at all. As you know, their new facilities were opened last year, and they are well placed for both laboratory and classroom space. The Arts students, however, are a different case. Students of History will now attend lectures in the newly opened Grenfell Hall. This applies to all the students: the whole faculty will teach in the Grenfell Complex, and, as I said before, major lectures will be in the Grenfell Hall. History students are all moving, but unfortunately their teachers will be left in the old building as the new office accommodation isn't yet ready. We hope to move some staff from the History Department within three months, but it will depend upon the availability of space. Better news for the engineers. Your faculty, staff and students, are already in the process of moving to the new campus. The structures lab is already in operation. The move for the engineers should be complete next week. The old Engineering Building will be taken

over by the Philosophy Department. The old structures lab has been gutted, and will be a small lecture hall. Work should be complete next summer in time for the new university year. The Faculty of Law has been moved downtown. As you know, this has been an on-going process for some time and it is now complete. The last books from the law library were put on their new shelves at the weekend. This leaves the premises previously occupied by the lawyers vacant. The planning committee is accepting suggestions for the way the building could be used. We'd like, if possible, to keep it as a public space: there has been a suggestion that it might be used as an art gallery or museum.

LISTENING 15

Narrator: Activity 15: 'Listening for Distinguishing Features'. Listen and write A, B, C or D to indicate which picture is being discussed.

1

Teacher: I want you to look at the triangles and find the one where both the inner and outer triangles are drawn with broken lines.

2

Man: Which flower do you like?

Woman: They're all pretty, but I like the one with four petals best.

3

Lecturer: Now here we have four excellent specimens of cactus. They're all fine and healthy, but the best of them is the one with the single stem which divides into three branches.

4

Police Officer: The missing girl is young. She has long hair, and when she was last seen she was wearing it in one pigtail falling over her shoulder.

5

Woman: Oh dear! I think Mr Lee has broken his glasses! They're lying here with one lens badly cracked.

LISTENING 17

Narrator: Activity 17: 'Swallow Life Insurance'. You will hear a conversation between a representative of an insurance company and a person who wishes to apply for life insurance. While you listen to the conversation, complete the person's application form.

Interviewer: Now, to process your application I need some details about you and about your medical history. Could you tell me your name, please?

George: Yes, my name is Rowlands, that's R-O-W-L-A-N-D-S, George Rowlands.

Interviewer: Thank you. And your address, Mr Rowlands?

George: I live in Strathfield, at 52 Green Street. The postcode for Strathfield is 2135.

Interviewer: Strathfield 2135. Thank you. How old were you at your last birthday?

George: I was 35 on September the 10th.

Interviewer: How tall are you, Mr Rowlands?

George: Um, I think I'm about 170 or 175 centimetres tall. Let's say one metre seventy-five.

Interviewer: And is your current weight your normal weight?

George: Oh yes, my weight doesn't change much. I suppose I'm lucky, really. I've never had to worry about putting on weight. I'm always about the same, around 80 kilos.

Interviewer: Fine. Are you married at the moment, Mr Rowlands?

George: Actually, that's one of the reasons I wanted to sort out some insurance. I'm planning to get married quite soon. I guess when you settle down you start to think of things like that.

Interviewer: Yes, we often find people take out life insurance when some major change happens in their lives, like getting married or changing their job. Now, I've got some questions relating to health matters. We will of course be requiring a full medical examination but I need some basic details from you now.

George: That's OK. I expect you need to know that I'm healthy, don't you?

Interviewer: That's right. Have you ever had a serious illness at any time of your life?

George: What would you describe as a serious illness?

Interviewer: Oh, not childhood things like measles, or a bad cold, but a kidney disorder, say, or pneumonia, or a cancerous growth.

George: Oh no, I've never had anything like that. I've always been healthy, never been in hospital.

Interviewer: I'll just write 'none' then. And I'll put the same thing, 'none', for major operations too, if you've never been in hospital. Do you have any medical conditions requiring medication?

George: No, not really. I take aspirin for a headache at times, but that's all. Oh, I guess you had better mention hay fever. I get bad hay fever in the early summer, and I take anti-histamines then.

Interviewer: Yes, I'd better note down 'hay fever'. Now, what about your parents? It's usually relevant to a person's medical history. Can you tell me if your parents are still alive?

George: My mother is still living, and she's healthy, but my father was killed last year in a car accident.

Interviewer: I'm very sorry to hear that. It must have been a shock to you.

George: Yes, it was a bad time for the whole family. He had just retired from his job and was looking forward to doing all sorts of things. He was only 67.

Interviewer: It's terrible the way these things happen, isn't it? I've just got one last question, Mr Rowlands. Do you smoke?

George: No, I don't smoke now. I used to, but I gave it up about 5 years ago.

Interviewer: Well, I think that's all for now. Thank you, Mr Rowlands. We'll let you know the date and time of your appointment for the medical checkup, and after that we can finalise your application.

George: Thank you very much. I'll wait to hear from you.

LISTENING 18

Narrator: Activity 18: 'Earthquakes'.

Newsreader: An earthquake struck Mexico's Pacific coast yesterday, killing at least 34 people and injuring more than 100. The destruction was greatest in the state of Colima, where a hotel collapsed in the earthquake. Last night it was confirmed that eight people had been killed in the collapse of the hotel and more were still trapped in the rubble. Emergency workers were using cranes and earthmoving equipment to try to locate hotel employees and guests still believed to be in the wreckage. Communications with the area were difficult as most services were cut by the quake, but telephone services were reopened late last night, and electricity supplies are slowly returning. Many roads were cut in the north part of the state where the damage was most severe. Hospitals in the area are believed to be coping with the emergency, and medical teams are being flown in by helicopter from Mexico City to assist in the disaster. The earthquake measured 7.6 on the Richter scale. Officials said that had the epicentre of the quake been closer to a more populated area such as Mexico City, the toll in lives would have been greater. Mexico City itself suffered a series of earth tremors several days earlier.

LISTENING 21

Narrator: Activity 21:

1. 'Sydbourne Earthquake'.

Newsreader: An earthquake measuring 6.5 on the Richter scale caused widespread damage to the northern areas of Sydbourne last night, striking around 10.30 pm, Eastern Standard Time. Fire Department officials said that three thousand buildings were completely demolished, while hundreds of fires started when electricity cables were brought down, causing short circuits. A State of Emergency was declared in

Sydbourne as gas mains throughout the northern suburbs ruptured, causing massive explosions and fireballs that could be seen 80 kilometres away, illuminating the city horizon. Authorities reported that by this morning most of the fires had been brought under control. However, damage to buildings is so severe that hundreds and possibly thousands of people are still trapped under tons of debris. Emergency crews say there is a shortage of heavy rescue machinery and they are powerless to rescue the victims of the quake. Some sections of major highways have been damaged, to the point where they are all but impassable. A witness who survived the collapse of her house said that it was the worst earthquake in living memory. Other residents in her area were not so lucky. At least ninety per cent of the downtown area resembles the scene of a nuclear disaster. The latest quake followed a series of minor tremors reported last Friday by the Centre for Seismic Research. A spokesperson for the Centre said that despite the repeated warning issued by the Centre to government authorities, the government failed to inform the media, with the result that warnings to evacuate the city were not issued. The spokesperson said that this negligence would now be paid for in human lives. Hilary Hughes, reporting from Sydbourne Emergency Co-ordination Centre, Sydbourne, for ILTC RADIO NEWS.

2: 'Storm lashes Sydney'.

Newsreader: Severe storms hit the western areas of the city last night, leaving scenes of destruction and at least a hundred homes without power or running water. Dozens of families were left homeless when the roofs of their houses were ripped away. Many of the areas hit were the same ones badly affected by hailstorms last week. In Macquarie Street, the council car park was completely flooded. A Toyota Corolla was badly damaged by floodwaters which carried the car across the carpark and into a large stormwater drain. A separate storm raced through the Federation Botanical Park. It uprooted at least fifty trees; many of them were over a hundred years old. In Menai, several trees were found lying on parked cars, causing an insurance bill that will run into the tens of thousands of dollars. Winds were recorded at speeds of over seventy kilometres an hour. People were trapped in cars for up to an hour because the floodwaters had left them stranded in swollen creeks, amidst a sea of debris. There were reports of cars being piled one on top of the other. In Lucas Heights a tree fell on a mini-bus that was taking the local soccer team to training. Luckily all but the driver escaped serious injury. The driver is in a satisfactory condition in Westmead Hospital. For tomorrow, weather reports predict improved conditions, with clear skies and an expected maximum temperature in the city of 14. Helen Brookes reporting for ILTC RADIO NEWS.

LISTENING 22

Narrator: Activity 22: 'Enrolment Day'. You will hear part of an introductory talk by a Student Information Officer. As you listen, answer Questions 1 to 7. Circle the correct answer.

Speaker: Welcome to the Orientation Program. I hope you are all settling in to your new residences and starting to feel at home here. This Orientation Program is designed to familiarise you all with some of the essential information about the University and about what it is like to be a student here, but before we begin I'd like to say a few words about enrolment day because I know that many students ... many of you are unsure of the procedures. There are two enrolment days, for different categories of student. Local students, or students who are permanent residents will enrol on the 16th of February. Overseas students will enrol two days later, on the 18th of February, in one of two sessions. First of all, all students doing undergraduate studies must come and enrol in the morning session. That morning enrolment session, for people enrolling in undergraduate courses, will be from 9.30 to 12.30 on Level 6 of the Walsh Building, in Room C 658. The Walsh Building is the one where the Faculty of Law is located. So that's for undergraduate students. Postgraduate students must also come to the same place, Room C 658 on Level 6, from 1.30 pm on the 18th, and that enrolment session finishes at 4.30 pm. When you come to enrol, and this applies to all students, please bring your passport or some other identification, that's really essential, and also bring the letter of acceptance from the Faculty you will be enrolling in. For overseas students we'll also need proof of your English proficiency level, that is, your IELTS test results, that's if you're an overseas student, and your health-care cards for health insurance, plus the receipt from the Student Admissions Office to show you have paid your fees. If there's anyone who hasn't paid their fees for this semester yet, please go to the Student Admissions Office and pay the fees as soon as possible. Your place at the university is not guaranteed until you've paid your fees and you cannot enrol. Just a word of advice: it's best to get a bank cheque to pay your fees. The thought of carrying $10,000 in cash in your pocket is terrifying. You could easily lose it or have it stolen. On Enrolment Day you'll all be issued with your Student Cards. You don't have to bring a photo for these. The enrolling officer will take an instant photo, and put it on the card with your student ID number and then laminate the card, so it's all done at once. You use this student card to borrow from the library,

PREPARE FOR IELTS: Skills and Strategies   INSEARCH ENGLISH

TRANSCRIPTS & ANSWERS

Listening Transcripts

to use student services like the medical centre, and even get discounts at the cinema and bookstores. By the way, the library hours are from 9.00 to 4.00 at the moment, but when the university term begins on the 21st of February the library opening times will be from 8.30 in the morning until 9.00 at night. It's also open at weekends. Okay? So, if you're all ready, we'll begin our tour of the campus now.

LISTENING 23

Narrator: Activity 23: 'Heathrow Airport Information'. Listen to this information about London Heathrow Airport. Write no more than three words for each answer.

Speaker: This information about London Heathrow Airport is provided by British Airways. There are four terminals at London Heathrow. Terminal One deals with all domestic flights within the United Kingdom. British Airways do not use Terminal Two. British Airways flights to Philadelphia use Terminal Three. All other British Airways intercontinental flights use Terminal Four. This includes the service on Concorde. If you are connecting flights with an airline other than British Airways, please ensure you follow the signs to your correct terminal. Travelling time between terminals is ten minutes by coach. A moving walkway connects Terminal One to Terminal Two. You should allow between 45 and 75 minutes between flights. On arrival, follow the signs to Flight Connections. Passengers who do not hold a boarding pass should report to the Flight Connections Centre. The Flight Connections Centre is located between Terminals One and Two. It contains a lounge of 600 seats, a children's play area, and, for a small charge, an executive-style lounge has secretarial support, shower facilities and sleeper seats in a quiet area. Central London is 15 miles to the east of the airport. There are several ways to travel there: taxi, bus, London underground and the Heathrow Express. A taxi will cost approximately 35 pounds, and is licensed to carry four passengers. The journey will take approximately 40 minutes. If you prefer to use the bus, Airbus Heathrow Shuttle has twenty-three Central London stops. The fare is six pounds for an adult travelling one way. Or you may take the London Underground served by the Piccadilly line. The trains depart approximately every five minutes, and the journey takes about 55 minutes. Or the Heathrow Express travels non-stop to London Paddington every 15 minutes. This journey takes approximately 15 minutes, and there are check-in facilities for customers with hand luggage only. We hope you enjoy your stay in the U.K., and look forward to serving you again.

LISTENING 24

Narrator: Activity 24: 'Student Counsellor's Talk'. Listen and complete the sentences below. Write no more than three words for each answer.

Speaker: Good morning everyone. This is the second of my three introductory talks as Overseas Student Counsellor at the university. In the first session you will remember we talked about the services offered in the Overseas Students' Unit at the university, and in this session I'd like to talk to you briefly about some of the problems, the most common problems that overseas students encounter when they come to study with us. After all, it's no secret that you may not find everything as easy as you would like, and we are here to help you. Firstly I'd like to talk about the transition experienced by many students from euphoria to doubt and depression. When students arrive they are usually excited by being in a new city with lots of attractions. Many students also enjoy the personal freedom of being in a foreign country, of meeting new friends and so on. But then when classes start and the student feels under pressure to hand in assignments, complete all the reading, understand the differences in learning style and everything else, they may begin to feel very unsure of their ability to cope and even wonder if they have made the right decision to come and study here. This depression phase that many students experience can be put down in the first place to simply being away from everything you are accustomed to. Being homesick is a natural thing to experience. Even students from this country whose family live in other cities experience homesickness. As part of missing home, many students find it hard to look after themselves, cooking, cleaning, shopping, paying bills, doing the laundry, things they might never have had to do before. It's part of learning to be independent, and to overcome it, try to make friends with other students from your own country and also with students in your classes; you'll be in class with them for a very long time so it's worth developing friendships here to make you feel more at home. The second factor that may be at the heart of depression is one that needs to be looked at carefully. Many students achieve low marks at first, low grades for academic work, and this is a problem that all students might experience, not just overseas students. Students often come to university with very high expectations; they are used to being high achievers, to doing very well at school, so their expectations are too high when they move to a completely different learning environment. In fact, this new learning environment should not be underestimated as a cause of low grades. Students may be using a different language, they may be required to work independently for the first time. Many of you will have to

TRANSCRIPTS & ANSWERS

153

present seminars, something you may never have done before in academic studies, and to do independent library research. You have to develop skills for this different style of learning, before you can achieve good grades. So, to cope with this possibly huge swing in your emotional state from excitement to very low morale, my advice in this first semester of your academic life is: be realistic about what you can achieve. If your expectations are too high you may become very depressed if you do not receive the grades you expect. A realistic approach is more sensible.

LISTENING 25

Narrator: Activity 25: 'Library Tour'. Listen to the guided tour commentary and label the places marked. Choose from the box below. Write the appropriate letters A to J on the diagram.

Librarian: Welcome to the library tour. We'll begin our tour of this level of the library here at the entrance. Then we'll go in a clockwise direction. So, first of all, over here on the left, next to the entrance, is a touch-screen information service; these computers can be used at any time to get general information about the library and how it works. In front of the touch-screen information service are the catalogues. As you can see it's a computerised catalogue system and it's very easy to use. The catalogues are linked up to the other libraries at the university, so make sure you check which library a book is in when you are trying to locate a particular item. Next, along here on the left, we have the Circulation Desk for borrowing and returning books. The Returns Area, the place for returned books and other items is at the end of the Circulation desk near Closed Reserve. Closed Reserve, as most of you probably know, is a collection of books that are in high demand so they are on restricted circulation. If a book is on Closed Reserve you can only borrow it to use within the library for three hours at a time. Over there in the corner are the shelves for newspapers. The library has an extensive collection of local and international English-language newspapers. They are kept on those shelves for one month and then stored elsewhere. As we continue our tour around to the right this large central section is the Reference Section. Reference texts cannot be borrowed for use outside the library; they must be used within the library. All these shelves in the centre of this level are the Reference Section. Now, the stairs here on the left lead to Level 2 only. On Level 2 are most of the Law books. To go up to the other levels of the library you have to use the lifts. Beside the stairs are the restrooms for this floor. Now, as we walk around this corner to the right, this large room on the left is the Audio-Visual Resource Centre. You can come

in here if you wish to listen to a tape or watch one of the library's videos. Next to the Audio-Visual Resource Centre is the photocopying room. There are 15 copiers for student use, and we've recently added a colour copier. The system for copying uses cards not coins. You can buy a photocopy card from the technician in charge of the photocopying room, or from the information desk if he isn't here at the time. On our right, these work tables are for student use, especially for small groups to work together, or you and your colleagues can use the conference room, which is that small room there next to the lockers. You can work on group projects in the conference room without disturbing anyone, and there's a conference room on each level of the library. The round desk in front of the lockers is the Information Desk. If you need help using the catalogues or you need to organise a loan from another library the information desk is the place to come. And finally, here, beside the exit doors, these two shelves contain current magazines and journals. Like the newspapers they are kept here for a time and then stored elsewhere. Okay, that's the end of the tour of this level of the library. I'll leave you to look around yourselves now, and if you need any further help please ask at the Information Desk.

LISTENING 26

Narrator: Activity 26: 'The Video Shop'. Robert has just bought a video recorder, and wants to hire movies from the local video shop. The manager is asking him for personal details to fill out the application form. Listen, and answer Questions 1 to 10.

Manager: Ok, could I have your full name, please?

Robert: Yes. My first name is Robert, R-O-B-E-R-T, Wutherspoon, W-U-T-H-E-R-S-P-O-O-N.

Manager: Could you repeat your surname, please?

Robert: Sure. Wutherspoon, W-U-T-H-E-R-S-P-O-O-N.

Manager: Good. Now, where do you live?

Robert: My address is 9809 Richmond, Apartment E 66, Houston, Texas, 77042.

Manager: Richmond is spelt R-I-C-H-M-O-N-D, right?

Robert: That's right. And it's Houston, Texas, 77042.

Manager: Right. Your contact number?

Robert: Yes, it's 795 (pause) 5183.

Manager: Is that at home or is it your work number?

Robert: That's my home number. My work number is 743 (pause) 3027.

Manager: And your date of birth is...?

Robert: December 6, 1979.

Manager: Good. Now I'll have to see some proof of identity. Do you have a driver's license or a passport with you?

Robert: Yes, I've brought my driver's license.

Manager: Thank you. Okay, I'll just record your license number: 1361 7844. You need to give me a password to authorise borrowing as well. What would you like as a password?

Robert: 'Horace'. It's my cat's name so I'll remember it easily.

Manager: Okay. Well, here's your license, and if you'll just wait a few minutes I'll laminate your membership card.

LISTENING 27

Narrator: Activity 27: 'The Bicycle Pump and Tyre Valve'. Listen to the conversation and label the parts of the bicycle pump and tyre valve. Write no more than two words for each answer.

Man: Why are these things always harder to describe than they are to use?

Woman: What do you mean?

Man: Well, I bet you know how to use a bicycle pump.

Woman: Of course. You use the bicycle pump to push air into your bicycle tyre.

Man: That's right. But I have to label these parts for an advertisement.

Woman: Let's have a look. Hmm. You could start with the handle. You could say something like 'The handle is easy to grip'.

Man: That's good. Now the pump body, which is drawn cut away so we can see inside it.

Woman: Maybe you could say 'The cylindrical pump body is made of durable material.'

Man: And then I could go on: 'The plunger in the centre of the pump body has a disc at the end of it...'

Woman: Hang on. You mean that big piece at the bottom of the plunger that looks as though it takes up all of the space inside the pump body? You could talk about how neatly the disc fits.

Man: That's right. Then I could go on about the air hose. You can see it connects the screwed hole at the bottom of the pump body and goes to the tyre valve.

Woman: I see. The air goes through the air hose into the tyre valve – that's that whole thing between the hose and the tyre.

Man: It's bracketed together on the diagram.

Woman: Yes, but there's one little piece that's labelled separately. Is it important?

Man: Hmm. Oh, oh, I see. It's the valve core. That's where the air goes before it's forced into the

valve. You can see where the rubber sleeve keeps the air in the tyre.

Woman: It's a really neat, simple design, isn't it?

Man: Yeah. Been around a while, too.

LISTENING 28

Narrator: Activity 28: 'Book Sales'. You will hear a talk about book sales in the University Book Stores. As you listen, answer questions 1 to 6 by completing the table showing the type of books sold in greatest numbers at the different University Book Stores.

Manager: Today I want to give you a breakdown of our sales in the different university bookstores across the campus. We've had some interesting results. We've used figures which show the number of books sold, not their dollar value. This is to screen out those very expensive technical books. Let's start in 1997. The bookstore in the Humanities Building sold hundreds of novels, but the major sales, by far the greatest number, were of general interest books. This result was probably to be expected. On the other hand, we were very surprised by the results we obtained in the Engineering Building, where we fully expected that most of the sales would be in technical books, and then found that they were in fact selling more novels than any other category. The question had to be asked: why is this so? We found there was a heavy trade among the students in second-hand technical books, and also there was serious competition from a cut-price bookseller who supplied from a van just off the university campus, so those two factors would have kept our technical book sales down, but they don't explain why novels were the top seller. The bookstore in the School of Nursing in 1997 also mainly sold novels, with technical books a distant second. The Sports Centre sold marginally more general interest books than anything else. And so we come to 1998. The bookstore in the Humanities Building sold more novels than ever before, edging out the general interest books two to one. The Engineering Building bookstore is still not selling as many technical books as one would wish; their main sales in 1998 were in general interest books. The store in the School of Nursing once again sold novels and very little else. The Sports Centre saw a return to the technical books – 80% of their sales in fact – with a popular series of Sports Medicine books which came out early in 1998. These results from 1997 and 1998 have taught us that we have to be competitive in technical books. Now, as to the future ....

LISTENING 29

Narrator: Activity 29: 'Matching to Illustrations'. Listen and write A, B, C or D to indicate the illustration being discussed.

1

Speaker 1: These graphs show the grain sales in this state. The graph for our particular area shows that we sold almost equal amounts of corn and barley – large amounts, in fact. We also sold equal amounts of wheat and rice, but we sold much less of these grains.

2

Speaker 1: The house I want you to look at has two stories and five windows downstairs.

Speaker 2: Does it have a chimney?

Speaker 1: Yes, it does. There's a little bit of smoke coming out. And it has six windows upstairs.

3

Speaker 1: Have you seen my mug?

Speaker 2: What does it look like?

Speaker 1: Well, it's a mug, it has no saucer.

Speaker 2: Does it have a lid?

Speaker 1: Yes. I left the lid sitting next to it.

Note: Answers to activities are given with acceptable alternatives indicated by /.

Unit One Listening

There is a Listening Answer Sheet on page 62 that may be used to record answers to the activities.

ACTIVITY 1

1 Four ✓

2 1 or 2 minutes; 4 or 5 minutes ✓

3 30 seconds; 30 seconds; you only hear the tape once

4 getting ready to start a course/checking in at a hotel or a dorm/asking for directions/arranging to meet people ('survival situation'); part of a lecture/(introducing) library facilities/ (explaining about) getting a student card ('academic situation')

5 British/Australian/American/Canadian

6 One person talking; Two people talking/ conversation between two people

7 using graphic information/pictures to choose/fill in a chart, table or form/multiple choice/short answers/fill in gaps

8 meaning

9 Listening Answer Sheet

ACTIVITY 2

1 15/5 or 5/15 or 15th May etc. (any correct form of the date is acceptable)

2 twice a day

3 recreation

4 1

5 2

6 3

7 2

8 4

ACTIVITY 3

Pronunciation of final sounds /t/, /d/ or /ɪd/

worked → /wɜkt/
pointed → /ˈpɔɪntɪd/
moved → /muvd/
visited → /ˈvɪzətɪd/
bored → /bɔrd/
wanted → /wɒntɪd/
danced → /dænst/ or /danst/
loved → /lʌvd/
stopped → /stɒpt/
thanked → /Θæŋkt/
attracted → /əˈtræktɪd/
laughed → /laft/
wished → /wɪʃt/
hated → /heɪtɪd/
mended → /mɛndɪd/

Pronunciation of final consonants

wash /wɒʃ/ → watch /wɒtʃ/
think /Θɪŋk/ → thing /Θɪŋ/
dead /dɛd/ → death /dɛΘ/
wish /wɪʃ/ → which /wɪtʃ/
sum /sʌm/ → sun /sʌn/
face /feɪs/ → phase /feɪz/

Pronunciation of numbers ending in –teen and –ty

60 – six**ty**	16 – six**teen**
90 – nine**ty**	19 – nine**teen**
1880 – eigh**teen** eigh**ty**	1818 – eigh**teen** eigh**teen**
50 – fif**ty**	15 – fif**teen**
80 – eigh**ty**	18 – eigh**teen**
1770 – seven**teen** seven**ty**	1717 – seven**teen** seven**teen**
40 – for**ty**	14 – four**teen**
70 – seven**ty**	17 – seven**teen**
1660 – six**teen** six**ty**	1616 – six**teen** six**teen**
30 – thir**ty**	13 – thir**teen**
1990 – nine**teen** nine**ty**	1919 – nine**teen** nine**teen**
1550 – fif**teen** fif**ty**	1515 – fif**teen** fif**teen**

ACTIVITY 3.1

1 0.75 (nought point seven five)/75% (seventy-five per cent)

2 0.6 (nought point six)/60% (sixty per cent)

3 3rd May

4 1/20 (one twentieth)/5% (five per cent)

5 0.5 (nought point five)/50% (fifty per cent)/a half

6 half past three

ACTIVITY 4

1 15

2 bent

3 led

4 work

5 60

6 ditch

7 bet

8 13

9 seal

10 slim

Listening Answers

ACTIVITY 5
1 1175
2 9555 6140
3 0055 12370
4 131 500
5 1 800 666 9181
6 672 3000
7 13 13 50
8 973 7333
9 43 1 201 316 809
10 1 800 025 121

ACTIVITY 6
1 21/21st March 1685 or 21/3/1685 or 3/21/1685
2 10/10th April or April 10/10th or 10/4 or 4/10
3 Feb./February 21/21st or 21/2 or 2/21
4 90s or nineties or 90's
5 30/30th Sept./September or 30/9 or 9/30
6 8/8th Nov./November or 8/11 or 11/8
7 16th century or C16
8 Nov./November 1853 or 11/1853
9 Dec./December 1/1st, 1950 or 1/12/1950
   or 12/1/1950
10 14/14th July or 14/7 or 7/14

ACTIVITY 6.1
$1/3$ – one-third
$3/4$ – three-quarters
$1/2$ – one-half/a half
$1/4$ – one-quarter/a quarter
$5/8$ – five-eighths
$7/5$ – seven-fifths

ACTIVITY 6.2
100% – one hundred per cent/a hundred per cent
2% – two per cent
20% – twenty per cent
5.5% – five point five per cent
10% – ten per cent
110% – one hundred and ten per cent/a hundred and ten per cent

ACTIVITY 6.3
0.5 – nought point five
71.95 – seventy-one point nine five
48.16 – forty-eight point one six
3046.20 – three thousand and forty six point two oh (or zero)
9652.44 – nine thousand six hundred and fifty-two point four four
.25 – point two five
93.5 – ninety-three point five

ACTIVITY 6.4
SW 1 – S-W one
W 9 – W nine
200072 – two thousand seventy-two
5097 – five oh nine seven
HARTSW 95 – H – A – R – T – S – W nine five
CA 3051 – C-A three zero five one
R2W 0M5 – R two W zero/oh M five
2088 – two oh double eight
3001 – three thousand one

ACTIVITY 6.5
RMB – China
EUR – The European Union
JPY – Japan
AUD – Australia
USD – The United States
GBP – Great Britain
INR – India
SAR – Saudi Arabia

ACTIVITY 7
1 $2/3$ or two-thirds
2 $12^{1/2}$% or 12.5%
3 $50
4 $5/8$ (five-eighths)
5 38.65%
6 £750
7 2.2
8 0.3%
9 $530 million
10 85.5% or $85^{1/2}$%

ACTIVITY 8
fountain – f-o-u-n-t-a-i-n
Belleville – capital B-e-double l-e-v-i-double l-e
Heathrow – capital H-e-a-t-h-r-o-w
Eileen McCulsky – capital E-i-l-double e-n; capital
  M-small c- capital C-u-l-s-k-y
giraffe – g-i-r-a-double f-e (g = /dʒi/)
Houston – capital H-o-u-s-t-o-n
Tasmania – capital T-a-s-m-a-n-i-a
laboratory – l-a-b-o-r-a-t-o-r-y
cafeteria – c-a-f-e-t-e-r-i-a
Jeffrey – capital J-e-double f-r-e-y (j = /dʒeɪ/)

ACTIVITY 9
1 Missouri
2 Canberra
3 Harry Luske
4 Johannesburg
5 Vancouver
6 (Maria) Strella
7 (Bill) McLean
8 Sammy's
9 Runnymede
10 (Professor) Kumar

ACTIVITY 10
1 C
2 D
3 A

ACTIVITY 11

Hair	Clothing
curly bald long spiky	casually dressed quite formal stylish

Height	Body Shape
fairly tall smallish average	plump slim overweight medium build thin

ACTIVITY 12
1 C
2 H
3 B
4 G
5 E
6 A
7 F
8 D

ACTIVITY 13
1 Calvi
2 Mario
3 Italian
4 German
5 more than 7
6 Post-graduate
7 13/8 or 8/13 or 13th August
8 30/8 or 8/30 or 30th August

ACTIVITY 13.1
1 popular
2 famous
3 well-known
4 accident
5 disaster
6 doctor's surgery/medical clinic
7 hospital

ACTIVITY 13.2
1 describing future possibilities
2 giving opinions
3 making suggestions
4 expressing necessity

ACTIVITY 13.3
2015 – in the future
2000 – a few years ago
Nine o'clock today – this morning
Nine o'clock tonight – this evening

ACTIVITY 13.4

Past	Present	Future
the day before yesterday earlier today ago last night later that day a few days later after we finished in 2003 during the year after a few months earlier today a week ago last century in the last 25 years a few days ago the other day	now right now	in a fortnight later in the week going to this evening this weekend in a month's time in the next decade by the end of the year in a day's time in the next decade in a year's time later in the year in a minute shortly in a moment

ACTIVITY 14

Note: Remember that True/False questions are not used in the IELTS Listening Test.

1 T
2 T
3 F
4 F
5 T
6 T
7 T
8 T
9 T

ACTIVITY 15

1 D
2 B
3 B
4 B
5 B

ACTIVITY 16

Person A

1 Where do I go to enrol?
   Enrolments are in Room Q50.
2 Where can I find the Careers Adviser?
   The Careers Adviser is located in Room F9940.
3 Where do I pay fees?
   Fees can be paid at the cashier in Room K33.
4 Is C130 the lecture room?
   No, the Lecture Room is J15.

5 Which room is Medical Services?
   Medical Services are located on Level 2 in Room V14.

Person B

6 Where can I find the Student Adviser?
   The Student Adviser is in Room D70.
7 Where do I enrol for Business Studies?
   Business Studies is in Room C19.
8 Where can I make a photocopy?
   Photocopies can be made in Room 2 on the 3rd floor.
9 Where is the professor's secretary?
   The professor's secretary is located on Level 16 in Room G90.
10 Where do I pay library fines?
   Library fines can be paid at the circulation desk located on the ground floor.

ACTIVITY 17

1 George Rowlands (surname must be spelt correctly)
2 52 Green Street, 2135
3 175 centimetres/1 metre 75 (cm)
4 80 kilos/80 kg
5 Single
6 None
7 None
8 Hay fever
9 Mother: yes; Father: no
10 Father: 67; Cause of death: car accident
11 No

ACTIVITY 18
√ disaster, √ destruction, √ collapsed, √ rubble, √ epicentre, √ earth tremors, √ trapped, √ Richter scale, √ medical teams, √ emergency

1 Mexico's Pacific coast
2 hotel
3 at least 34 people
4 more than 100
5 cranes and earthmoving equipment
6 in the north part of the state
7 helicopter
8 7.6

ACTIVITY 19

TOPIC: PROBLEMS OF DEVELOPING COUNTRIES
Possible vocabulary

Adjectives	Nouns	Verbs
serious poor economic political industrial illiterate	**unemployment** **epidemics** **population growth** **poverty** **lack of resources** **famines** **disease** malnutrition overpopulation education literacy crime instability minorities life expectancy sanitation migration	to decline to increase to relate to to reduce to depend on to cause

TOPIC: POLLUTION
Possible vocabulary

Adjectives	Nouns	Verbs
environmental water chemical noise industrial air atmospheric	**environment** **CO2 emissions** **industrial waste** **toxic chemicals** control source problem legislation risk cost health impact	to cause to prevent to reduce to control

ACTIVITY 20
RESERVATIONS
Possible answers
1 holiday
2 Africa
3 I've been to every continent except Africa.
4 to go on a safari
5 expensive
6 $2,500
7 Tasmania and Queensland
8 has beautiful beaches

CLUB MEMBERSHIP
Possible answers
1 complete an application form
2 9:00 am and 5:00 pm
3 the Student Union Building
4 yourself
5 your interests
6 $20
7 attend at least 3 meetings a year
8 speak with the club secretary
9 horseback riding in the mountains

ACTIVITY 21
√ quake, √ rescue, √ collapse, √ evacuate, √ emergency, √ victims, √ ruptured, √ disaster, √ fireballs, √ powerless, √ debris, √ demolished, √ warning, √ shortage, √ electricity cables, √ trapped, √ minor tremors, √ Richter scale, √ brought down, √ explosions, √ rescue machinery, √ brought under control

ACTIVITY 21.1

Buildings	collapse, demolished, wreckage, rubble, debris
Power supplies	powerless, electricity cables, brought down
People	rescue, evacuate, medical teams, victims, trapped
Emergency crews	rescue, evacuate, medical teams, emergency, brought under control
Roads and highways	disaster, collapse

Synonyms
debris: wreckage, rubble
collapse: brought down

ACTIVITY 21.2

Before (an earthquake)	evacuate, emergency, tremors, warning, minor tremors
During	quake, rescue, medical teams, emergency, victims, disaster, tremors, fireballs, ruptured, trapped, minor tremors, brought down, explosions
After	wreckage, collapse, rubble, debris, powerless, demolished, electricity cables, minor tremors, Richter scale, rescue machinery, shortage, brought down, brought under control

ACTIVITY 21.3
Sydbourne earthquake
Correct Answers:
1 caused widespread damage/struck around 10:30 pm Eastern Standard Time
2 heavy rescue machinery
3 earthquake in living memory
4 series of minor tremors

ACTIVITY 21.4
Storm lashes Sydney
Correct Answers:
1 western areas of the city
2 floodwaters
3 over seventy kilometres an hour
4 mini-bus

ACTIVITY 22
1 D
2 B
3 C
4 A
5 B
6 B
7 C

ACTIVITY 23
1 (Terminal) 3
2 ten (10) minutes
3 Flight Connections Centre
4 four (4)
5 fifty-five (55) minutes

ACTIVITY 24
1 excited
2 homesickness/being homesick
3 (receiving/achieving) low grades/marks
4 high expectations/different learning environment
5 realistic

ACTIVITY 24.1
2 I'd like to talk to you about 1 Firstly
3 In the first place 4 The second factor
5 In fact 6 So

ACTIVITY 25
1 B
2 F
3 H
4 G
5 C
6 I
7 E
8 J
9 A
10 D

ACTIVITY 25.1
1 false
2 false
3 true
4 true
5 false
6 false
7 true
8 false
9 false

ACTIVITY 26
1 Robert (must have correct spelling)
2 Wutherspoon (must have correct spelling)
3 9809 Richmond (must have correct spelling)
4 E 66
5 Texas
6 795 5183
7 743 3027
8 6/12/1979 or 12/6/1979 or 6th December 1979 or December 6, 1979
9 (driver's) license (US)/licence (Brit.Australian)
10 1361 7844

ACTIVITY 27
1 handle
2 pump body
3 plunger
4 disc
5 screwed hole
6 air hose
7 tyre valve
8 valve core

ACTIVITY 28
1 N
2 N
3 G
4 N
5 N
6 T

ACTIVITY 29
1 C
2 B
3 A

Unit Two Speaking

ACTIVITY 1

Vocabulary	Synonym
leisure time	spare time; free time
apartment (American English)	flat (British English); unit
sister-in-law	husband's sister; wife's sister; brother's wife
niece	brother's daughter; sister's daughter; daughter of wife's brother/sister; daughter of husband's brother/sister
international student	overseas student; foreign student
homemade	do-it-yourself (DIY); handmade; homespun
snack food	light meal; bite (informal)
suburb	outskirts; borough; urban sprawl; district
sports game	match; a meet (especially, track meet)

ACTIVITY 2
1 first
2 next
3 second
4 Finally

ACTIVITY 3
1 While
2 when
3 was
4 Before
5 had
6 after
7 During
8 in the end
9 Just as
10 already

ACTIVITY 4
1 They
2 their
3 them
4 these
5 themselves
6 their
7 They
8 their
9 he
10 his

ACTIVITY 5
1 For example
2 Not only
3 also
4 so
5 but
6 Firstly
7 Moreover
8 Secondly
9 However
10 In brief
11 Although

ACTIVITY 6

1 but
2 Next
3 however
4 as
5 also

ACTIVITY 7

Phrases used to include additional information:
furthermore; in addition; on top of; what's more

ACTIVITY 8

1 different
2 but
3 Although/While
4 similar
5 differences
6 on the other hand
7 whereas
8 Although/While

ACTIVITY 9

1 similarities
2 similarity
3 similarly
4 Both
5 either

ACTIVITY 10

1 a case in point
2 in particular
3 by way of illustration
4 an example
5 For instance/For example
6 for example/for instance
7 such as

ACTIVITY 11

1 because
2 result
3 led to
4 meant
5 flow
6 means
7 as
8 resultant

ACTIVITY 12

1 I
2 G
3 A
4 B
5 H
6 C
7 F
8 J
9 D
10 E

ACTIVITY 13

Possible answers
1 name
2 work; a student
3 your home town
4 come from
5 been here

ACTIVITY 14

1 on
2 in
3 on
4 below
5 under
6 on
7 onto
8 from
9 Off
10 along
11 at
12 opposite
13 next
14 in
15 on

ACTIVITY 15

1 tiring; tired
2 stimulating; boring; bored; stimulated
3 fascinating; fascinated
4 embarrassing; embarrassed
5 frustrated; frustrating

ACTIVITY 16
1 like
2 for instance/for example
3 such as
4 a case in point
5 example
6 For example/For instance
7 namely
8 An illustration

ACTIVITY 17
1 wish
2 hopes
3 hope
4 wish
5 hoped
6 hope
7 hopes
8 wish
9 hope
10 wish

ACTIVITY 18
1 When
2 to return
3 will
4 might
5 job
6 Otherwise
7 could/might
8 option
9 position
10 Alternatively
11 goal
12 wish
13 would be

ACTIVITY 19
1 I imagine/It's likely
2 predict
3 I would guess that
4 in the next generation
5 guess
6 it's likely/I imagine

ACTIVITY 20
1 surprised
2 amazing
3 huge
4 excited
5 envious
6 enthusiastic
7 enjoying
8 interesting

ACTIVITY 21
1 more ... than
2 most
3 the same ... as
4 as many ... as
5 greater ... than
6 biggest
7 more ... than
8 not so many ... as; as much
9 least

ACTIVITY 22
1 in
2 in
3 in
4 at
5 ago
6 at
7 in
8 at
9 in
10 at
11 at
12 at
13 in
14 at

ACTIVITY 23
Strongest
1 Undoubtedly
2 I believe that ...
3 I expect that ...
4 I'm quite sure that ...
5 I'm fairly sure that ...
6 Probably
7 Possibly
8 Maybe/Perhaps
9 Perhaps/Maybe
10 There could be .../I guess that ...
11 I guess that .../There could be ...

ACTIVITY 24
1 should
2 I believe
3 could
4 couldn't
5 may
6 In my opinion
7 might
8 wouldn't

Remember:
may = permission
might = suggestion
can/could = ability

VOCABULARY GRID

Make a list of new words, organised by THEME. Find all the forms of each new word. Mark stressed syllables.

THEME:

| Adjective | Opposite | Noun | | | Verb | Adverb |
		Place	Person	Thing		

VOCABULARY GRID

Make a list of new words, organised by THEME. Find all the forms of each new word. Mark stressed syllables.

THEME:

		Noun				
Adjective	Opposite	Place	Person	Thing	Verb	Adverb

VOCABULARY GRID

Make a list of new words, organised by THEME. Find all the forms of each new word. Mark stressed syllables.

THEME:

Adjective	Opposite	Noun			Verb	Adverb
		Place	Person	Thing		

VOCABULARY GRID

Make a list of new words, organised by THEME. Find all the forms of each new word. Mark stressed syllables.

THEME:

Adjective	Opposite	Noun			Verb	Adverb
		Place	Person	Thing		

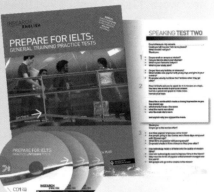

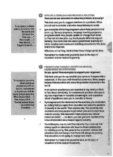